PRAISE FOR *MORE THAN A BAG*

Our most tenured Thirty-One Leaders share these words about the book.

"As the first Consultant, I have seen all the ups and downs of growing this amazing company. Thirty-One has changed thousands of lives across the world, and I am blessed to be part of it."

Jenny Hillenburg, Tennessee

"How fun to discover things from Cindy's perspective 'behind the scenes' while Thirty-One was in its infancy and becoming all that it is today!"

Libby Aulenbach, Pennsylvania

"Cindy Monroe is not the stereotypical corporate executive that pops into mind. Instead, she is a grassroots entrepreneur who has given her heart and soul around every turn to build Thirty-One to the brand it is today while helping her Consultants establish their own successful businesses. In *More Than a Bag*, you get a sneak peek into her experiences … both challenging and celebratory."

Neely Basich, Wisconsin

"*More Than a Bag* is such a blessing to read. How lucky am I to relive so many of my favorite Thirty-One moments and reflect on my own more than fifteen-year journey with Thirty-One."

Lori Benseler, Ohio

"Cindy Monroe changed my life with Thirty-One! I will be forever grateful for her vision, passion, persistence, and prayers over the years. Thirty-One is truly much more than a bag. I've been blessed to be a part of this journey in so many ways and can't imagine what my life would have been like without it."

Dawn Brown, Tennessee

"God gave Cindy this business to help cultivate the Proverbs 31 women and reach beyond just 'a bag.' Through her inspiration, I was and continue to be challenged to be the best me as a wife, mother, and successful business owner. Her leadership and friendship are unmatched!"

Deann Champagne, North Carolina

"What Cindy Monroe shares I have felt and known for years. Her vision has empowered women through her faith and dedication. I am blessed to be on this journey."
Jen Cornell, North Carolina

"The history of Thirty-One Gifts is so much better than a fairy tale. It is the story of a real person's dream and vision coming true, and the lives that were touched. *More Than a Bag* is that story captured in the pages of a book reminding me as a founding consultant of the wonderful real-life adventure I have been on with Cindy Monroe and Thirty-One Gifts."
Holley Cox, Tennessee

"This is the story of Cindy and Scott Monroe and their support for one another in the pursuit of building a business to empower women. This true journey shows their love for these women and their families through their training, inspiration, and keeping it real."
Angie DeLong, Nebraska

"I quickly realized that Thirty-One Gifts is more than a bag. It is a culture of women who support and encourage one another to be the BEST version of themselves."
Donna Duarte Strathroy, Ontario, Canada

"I could not stop reading this! Thirty-One has impacted women and families all over the world for twenty years, and this book let me relive so many great moments all over again. *More Than a Bag* leaves you feeling encouraged, hopeful, and more confident than ever to start chasing your dreams."
Kerrie Early, South Carolina

"Cindy takes you on a personal, behind-the-scenes journey in *More Than a Bag* that will leave you encouraged and inspired. I'm so grateful that God wrote Thirty-One into my story, and I have been blessed by Cindy and Scott over the years. Reading this book will give you a glimpse into just how special Thirty-One truly is."
Jackie Gerbers, Indiana

"A richly captivating behind-the-scenes story of Thirty-One. It was a delightful reminder and inspiring telling of the faith-filled business that turned into something bigger than anyone could have ever imagined."
Jonet Greenfield, Idaho

"Cindy has been incredibly inspirational by creating a positive impact that has resulted in helping women all around the country empowHER themselves and contribute towards their families.... and it all started with a simple monogram."

Ashley Haley, Florida

"I've witnessed firsthand over the last twelve years how Thirty-One has always been 'more than a bag.' Cindy's story and success provide women like myself with inspiration and drive to reach their full potential. A must-read!"

Lisa Harvey, Pennsylvania

"Cindy has captured the heart of Thirty-One when she writes that 'Thirty-One supports more than the material parts of life; it also supports the emotional parts of life.' I experienced this firsthand when our son died and the Sisterhood rallied, taking care of not just my business but also our family in countless ways. Our community still talks about how they showed up and loved us. There is nothing like the Thirty-One Sisterhood."

Catherine Hauschild, Ohio

"With a passion for celebrating and encouraging women, Cindy shares her heartfelt journey—one that changed the lives of hundreds of thousands of women. Her story is authentic, inspiring, and empowering, and it has truly been a gift to be part of this blessing."

Courtney Hawkins, Florida

"Being part of Thirty-One with Cindy for more than 15 years has been an incredible blessing. This book shows you how much strength and guidance Cindy and Scott pull from their faith in everything they do. Because of Thirty-One, my family has been able to do more, be more, and give more than ever before."

Suzanne Hudson, Georgia

"*More Than a Bag* is a wonderful journey through Cindy Monroe's legacy with Thirty-One. Being part of Thirty-One is definitely more than a bag, and this book captures that."

Danielle Johnson, Michigan

"In *More Than a Bag,* Cindy portrays what can happen when you follow your dream and, more important, the impact of teaching others how to be brave and follow their own dreams."

Lindsay Kahl, Illinois

"My mentor and friend Cindy Monroe is unapologetically an authentic Proverbs 31 woman. For thirteen years, she has taught me how to build a business while remaining true to faith and family. There is no better founder and no better business in the direct sales field."

Melissa Kaule, Florida

"I've always admired Cindy Monroe and how she has built this business from the 'basement' up. It was a joy to learn exactly what it took to get where we are today as a company, and I look forward to another twenty years. I thank God every night for bringing Thirty-One into my life and blessing my family."

Julie Leeds, New York

"As a mentee and friend of the Monroes, I love that this book reveals how authentic and powerful Scott and Cindy truly are. They have mastered the art of the forever struggle that is the work/life balance and helped so many discover their own 'why' on their journeys. I am proud to be part of the Thirty-One family, and I can't thank these two enough for helping me become the best version of me for my team, family, and friends."

Jennifer Lovelady, Ontario, Canada

"*More Than a Bag* is a delightful, easy-to-read memoir that highlights all the hard work, love, and perseverance that have made Thirty-One one of the top direct selling companies in the world."

Gretchen Manmiller, Pennsylvania

"Cindy shares how her vision came to life through her faith in God, hard work and perseverance. A truly inspirational message for those of us who have been a part of the journey."

Mariekan Martin, Virginia

"Cindy Monroe takes readers on her personal journey of building a business from her basement in rural Tennessee. So many people like me have been thankful and blessed to share and experience this journey. An inspiring and challenging story!"

Lynn McCutcheon, South Carolina

"Cindy Monroe's story is one of tenacity and perseverance. In *More Than a Bag,* readers get an inside look at what it took to build a business that has impacted the lives of countless women over the last two decades."

Amy Murray, Texas

"Cindy Monroe exemplifies faith, perseverance, and leadership as she shares stories about her journey building a successful faith-based company alongside her devoted husband, Scott. It is a true honor to be part of it all."

Lindsay O'Connor, Ontario, Canada

"Cindy Monroe chronicles how her mission to empower and encourage women led her to create a company that was *More Than a Bag*. Her passion for watching others grow shines through in this book. She takes us on her journey of creating a legacy by following God's plan, with a focus on her personal 'why' while encouraging others to know theirs. As she explains and I know personally, it was a strong sense of purpose that led her to create such a powerful impact."

Lynn Pfost, Kentucky

"*More Than a Bag* is an in-depth peek behind the curtain that reveals the true heart of Thirty-One. Cindy's honesty in telling her story has taken me back through my own journey with the company and reminded me why I started, why I'm still here, and what I have to look forward to. I found it so refreshing. Thirty-One truly is so much more than a bag."

Shea Politte, Texas

"Cindy Monroe has a gift for mentoring and reminding us that we can move mountains. I'm thrilled that the rest of the world gets to read about this journey that we are so very grateful to be on with her."

Cherie Rabern, Florida

"Cindy Monroe is a you-get-what-you-see kind of lady, and this is one of the many reasons she is so deeply respected, admired, and loved. Her passion for all that Thirty-One encompasses is never wavering. In *More Than a Bag*, that truth jumps out with every turn of the page. Thank you, Cindy, for the positive impact you've had on my family and team."

Julie Raby, Ontario, Canada

"In *More Than a Bag*, Cindy Monroe shares her heart through a collection of personal stories of encouragement and inspiration. Reading it reminded me of how she gave this non-dreamer not only permission to dream, but also permission to dream BIG! It blessed me all over again."

Kelly Ricketts, Florida

"Whether you are an entrepreneur looking for inspiration or someone who loves a great success story, Cindy Monroe's *More Than a Bag* is a heartfelt read that shares how she started a company for women out of prayers and a dream. Cindy's passion has always been helping others succeed, and here she unfolds the beautiful story and purpose of Thirty-One Gifts."
Donna Runion, Tennessee

"Cindy Monroe embodies the core values our company celebrates. I am proud of her as our founder, and I love sharing our mission to celebrate, encourage, and reward women and families. I love reading how far we've come in the last twenty years, and I am excited to see what is coming."
Kara Schmidt, Illinois

"Cindy Monroe shares how focusing on fulfilling a vision of empowering others enabled her to build a successful direct sales company unlike any other in the industry. Stories show how staying true to her 'why' while being grounded in faith and family impacted and blessed not only her own journey but also those of countless others, including me."
Kendra Schmit, Nebraska

"Cindy Monroe takes you inside the inspiring story of not only how Thirty-One came to be, but also what makes it so special. This book is a unique reflection on empowering stories about overcoming obstacles and making life-changing decisions. She captures the beauty of what being part of this family has meant to so many like myself."
Hope Shortt, Virginia

"I love how Cindy shows readers, the journey wasn't easy, but it was worth it. In the beginning, being open to constant change only kept supporting the kind of company she was determined to build. The values speak for themselves."
Amy Sorensen, South Dakota

"The adventurous, humble, and unexpectedly successful journey of Cindy Monroe and Thirty-One touched many lives, including mine, throughout these last twenty years. I'm not sure where we would be today without the incredible vision and leadership of Cindy and Scott."
Kaine Story, Alabama

"In *More Than a Bag*, Cindy Monroe shows how having a strong 'why' and living in your purpose are key to finding success in any area of life. Being part of the Thirty-One family for fifteen years and watching Cindy lead the company with such grace and strength has given me the confidence to live life on my own terms. I will be forever grateful."
Susan Sullivan, Kentucky

"*More Than a Bag* follows the epic journey of success of one of the greatest stories of entrepreneurship in recent history. It gives readers a chance to look through the lens of Cindy Monroe, a great American businesswoman who started in her basement and drove the Thirty-One Sisterhood to a nationally recognized symbol of what is possible if you dream big, work hard, and keep the faith."
Lindsay Tanner, Arizona

"Cindy Monroe has written a must-read for anyone who is looking to step out in faith and dream big. Read this book and learn from one of the best!"
Misty Thomas, Alabama

"Cindy Monroe continues to cast a vision that has made it possible for thousands of women to follow their dreams and make a difference in their homes, their communities, and the world."
Ja Thoms, Michigan

"Cindy's story of humble beginnings and explosive growth will transport you into the infamous 'Pink Bubble'... a special place I have loved for years."
Tyree Toohey, Kentucky

"A personally nostalgic read for me and an inspiration to all! As you read, you will be blessed to learn lessons for life and business."
Kirstin Tracy, California

"When I joined Thirty-One more than fifteen years ago, I had no idea about the journey I was about to embark on. This book captures the true spirit of the Sisterhood, the faith, and the values we all stand for. Thirty-One Gifts truly is so much more than great bags. My faith is stronger and my life is richer because of this journey. In true Thirty-One fashion, this book shares not only great business tips but also great life tips."
Bobbi Trisko, Minnesota

"Cindy Monroe shares with her readers what I believe is the biggest reason for the company's success: Our people, not our products, are our 'why.' From the beginning, Cindy and Scott made people the priority, and I'm proud to say that is still true today."
Tiffany Wellinghoff, Ohio

"*More Than a Bag* reveals exactly why Cindy Monroe has captured the hearts of so many over the years. She shares the mission, vision, and values of her company as well as the intimate stories of the heart that truly fueled others to be 'all in' on this incredible journey with her. This is a world-class story that will help you rethink the 'why' in your own life and business."
Jennifer Pasalakis Wessner, Tennessee

"I love reading the behind-the-scenes stories and God moments that have made Thirty-One such a success story. Thirty-One is not just a success in terms of such things as income, vacations, and friendships. More important, it is a success on a deeper, life-affirming, and Kingdom-building level that has impacted people for eternity, my family included. Thank you, Cindy Monroe and Thirty-One!"
Jennifer Westerhoff, Colorado

"Cindy's experience and wisdom are an incredible gift to others. She inspires everyone around her to make time for what matters most in order to create a happy and fulfilling life. This book will lift your heart and help you connect with your true purpose in life."
Nadine Willemse, Ontario, Canada

"A peek behind the curtain of an amazing journey I had no idea would shape my life and help me become the woman, wife, mother, and leader I am today."
Alexa Williams, Virginia

"Cindy Monroe is a true inspiration! Her vision and journey to empower and inspire women is something very special, and I got as much inspiration from this book as I still receive as a leader with Thirty-One."
Lisa Witherite, Ohio

MORE THAN A BAG

Celebrating the First 20 Years of the Thirty-One Story

CINDY MONROE
Founder of Thirty-One

WITH JULIE SUTTON & CATHY SMITH

More Than a Bag

Requests for information should be emailed to:
hello@cindymonroe.com

ISBN 978-1-955051-11-8 (softcover)
ISBN 978-1-955051-12-5 (ebook)

Cindy Monroe titles may be purchased in bulk for church, business, fundraising, or educational use. For information, please email hello@cindymonroe.com.

Cover and interior design: Erik M. Peterson

Published for the benefit of the Thirty-One Sisterhood.

First Printing 2022 / Printed in the United States of America

AUTHOR BIOS

CINDY MONROE founded Thirty-One Gifts in the basement of her Chattanooga, Tennessee, home in 2003 with a few friends. Today she continues to build relationships with Thirty-One sales Consultants all over the country and establish strategic plans to grow and expand the brand. Cindy serves on the Board of Directors for the Direct Selling Association and on the Advisory Board of Nationwide Children's Hospital of Columbus Foundation. Cindy's passion outside of her career is her beautiful family, husband, Scott, and children, Alyx and Evan.

JULIE SUTTON is the co-founder of Thirty-One Gifts. Today Julie continues to focus on the strategy and execution of all things sales-field focused at Thirty-One. She is the company historian as well as the Thirty-One Gives philanthropic torchbearer. Most recently, she served six years on the school board at Concord Christian School in Knoxville, Tennessee, where she has been grateful to use her business knowledge to contribute to her community. Julie's most valued partners in life are her husband, Jason, and her children, Jordan, Jacob, and Jozie.

CATHY SMITH is one of the "Founding Mothers" of Thirty-One Gifts. She was the first employee and is often referred to as the "heart" of the company. Cathy has served many roles at Thirty-One, including cheerleader, relationship-builder, peacekeeper, culture-keeper, and memory-maker. She is passionate about building relationships. Her top priority is her family, including her husband, Rodney, and children, Savannah, Dakota, and daughter-in-law, Maggie.

CONTENTS

AUTHOR'S NOTE

I avoided writing a book for many years. I always came up with excuses when people suggested I share our story. I finally came around to the idea, but I am choosing to be specific with my audience and stay on a "Thirty-One" path. You will read personal stories, but each one is tied to a supporter of this amazing company.

I am writing this for those who have been on the journey with me. To anyone who has ever worked as an employee or contractor to help us create this amazing story and every Consultant who has invested in this dream, this book is for you. To all who believed in me, our Consultants and employees, thank you for your faith and partnership during the highs and lows. You know who you are, and this book is for you.

While I do not consider this a business book, it is a place where any entrepreneur can find takeaways that worked well and pitfalls to avoid. Any direct selling Consultant/representative will find nuggets of what is important when running your own business. Finally, I believe everyone connected to Thirty-One can read this and stand tall together to celebrate the beautiful tradition we have built during our first 20 years.

Thank you for your grace and support as I put these words and stories on paper.

INTRODUCTION

The Reason Why

SOME PEOPLE THINK we empower women to sell bags, but the truth is we sell bags to empower women. I founded Thirty-One Gifts in 2003 with one simple goal in mind: to help women by giving them the opportunity to run their own successful businesses. That goal remains our No. 1 priority today. Not only do our fashionable, functional products make life easier, but they also help independent business owners support their families and reach their dreams. Over nearly two decades, our Consultants have held more than six million parties. Along the way, we've also been blessed to give back to organizations that share our mission of empowering girls, women, and families in North America and around the world.

We all have a *why*, a reason for doing the things we do. Maybe yours is family, friends, faith, or flexibility. Maybe it's just having fun. Our *why* is to help you reach yours. This book is the untold story of how we've done that. Together with Julie Sutton and Cathy Smith, I share the narrative backstory of how our journey led to the making of Thirty-One Gifts, one of the largest direct sales companies started in the last 20 years, with more than five-billion dollars in total sales at the time of this printing, 2003–2022. We have been called the "darling of the direct sales industry" and were once projected to be among the few direct sales companies to reach one billion dollars in annual sales (a target we have yet to reach). Our story, however, has not been without its ups and downs. Our most successful season was followed by one of declining sales. We are here today not because we built this company to be the best or make the most money, but because we built this company to empower women, like me and you.

In the pages ahead, you will read about many things we started in the beginning of our company that are alive and well today. We are still living out our amazing origin story and work culture as I write this, with many of our traditions and tools continuing to inspire both new and seasoned Consultants, leaders, customers, and friends of Thirty-One.

This book about our story is my love letter to the employees and Consultants at Thirty-One and a way to honor all who have been a part of this journey. There is a saying that "life is about the journey, not the destination," and I feel so blessed to have been on this journey with many of you who are reading this book. Thank you for coming along with me!

PART ONE

From Bootstraps to a Business

"Whether you think you
can or you can't,
you are right."

—HENRY FORD

1

FIRE

Follow the Spark

I WAS A DADDY'S GIRL when I was little. Moments spent by his side as a kid are memorialized in my mind. On one day I'll never forget my dad asked me to come outside for a chat. I knew *this time* I was not in trouble. He sat me down on the hillside by the house he hand-built in Soddy Daisy, Tennessee, and told me he was no longer going to live with us. After nine years of marriage, my parents were getting divorced. I'm not sure my six-year-old self understood what all that meant on that day, or what it would mean for the rest of the years ahead of us, but I love both my mom and dad so much. That would never change. We got to see Daddy on weekends until he got a job out of town, and then he faithfully called long-distance every Friday night to talk to me and my sister, Christie.

One Friday, Daddy called as I was about to get in the shower. I was butt-naked (or "butt-nekkid," as we say in the South), but I ran down the hall to the phone. You can bet your life I was not going to miss his call. "Hi, Daddy!" I said, out of breath. We talked for a few minutes, me standing there without clothes on, warm shower flowing as it fogged up the mirrors. Next thing I knew, smoke alarms were going off. Now, smoke alarms were a normal occurrence in our house, especially between the hours of 5:00 and 6:00 in the evening when my mom was making her nightly yummy dinner. It didn't seem out of the ordinary if there was something burning in the oven. So, I kept talking with Daddy and ignored the alarms.

A few minutes later, my mom started yelling for us to get out of the house. My mom was, and still is, one of the most bad-ass women I know, but yelling was what she did best in those early years. It took a few seconds for her words to register and for me to realize that *this* time, her yelling was for *real.* For heaven's sake, I was on the phone with Daddy! But Mom was yelling about a fire burning somewhere and saying we had to get out. "Daddy, I need to go. The house is on fire! Love you, bye!" I can only imagine how he felt halfway across the country, hanging up on his baby girl who just told him the house he'd hand-built was on fire, and the people he loved were on the run outside.

I dropped the phone and ran. When Mom saw my tiny naked body, she quickly grabbed a coat from the hallway closet as we dashed out the front door. It was dark, and the fastest way to our closest neighbor was through the woods. I was already an expert at running through the woods. It was where I spent my days, playing on my own and with friends. But that night, running as fast as I could with my mom and sister, I was scared. To make matters worse, sticks hurt my bare feet and I caught the arch of my foot on the pointed top of the chain-link fence as we climbed over it. But I had to outrun the pain. The next thing I remember, I was standing at my neighbor's side door while my mom frantically explained what happened. The fire department came and put out the fire, but it was months before we were able to return to our home.

The damage to the kitchen could be repaired. But what couldn't be healed was the loneliness and vulnerability I felt at a deep level in my six-year-old soul. I don't remember many more details from that night. I think I blocked most of it out. But I do remember being surrounded by my family and neighbors and still feeling completely alone. I don't recall any comforting hugs or words of reassurance from the adults or other kids who swarmed together that evening. We were all in survival mode. There was no one to blame. Accidents happen. But looking back, I realize that night has shaped my entire life.

Forty-plus years later, I can see how the boiling oil that set fire to our kitchen and the vulnerability and loneliness I felt in those frightful moments also lit a spark inside of me. Somehow, the message I absorbed from that night was that *I was the only one ultimately responsible for me.* Ever since, I've worked hard to make things happen, keep things under control, be on the lookout for problems to prevent or solve, and I always create a safe space for myself and the people around me.

Fast-forward to my late twenties. I had a full-time job, a husband, two small children, and a hand-built home of my own, when my best friend, Pam, invited me to go to a bead store to learn to make bracelets. I loved jewelry, but even more, I loved Pam. So, when she asked for a girls' night, I was all in. On several occasions, we'd travel to neighboring towns to visit bead stores for supplies. But in the summer of 2003, I asked my husband, Scott, to drive us to the Atlanta gift market, AmericasMart Atlanta, to see what beads I could find. Walking past the stalls of thousands of vendors fanned a tiny spark inside me, igniting another flame too big to ignore. We picked out beads, but I found so much more—gift items, like purse-shaped ceramic cookie jars and thermal tote bags. I grabbed catalogs, names, and numbers, not really sure what I would do with them.

When I got home, I couldn't get these products out of my mind. After discussing it with Scott, we came up with a business plan for a catalog-based company. I wasn't thinking of the long days and financial investment it would take to open a brick-and-mortar gift shop. I thought that if people bought such things as kitchen tools, baskets, and beauty products via catalogs, they would surely be interested in a curated collection of boutique gifts too. I immediately thought of our friends Jason and Julie Sutton to help. They joined in, and that August and September, Jason and I designed a gift catalog using photographs provided by vendors. Julie and I developed and executed the rest of the business plan. By October, we were holding that catalog in our hands.

Here's how Julie recalls our blossoming partnership:

> I first met Scott and Cindy when I was 12 years old. Scott was a mentor/leader for our school band. Cindy was a couple years ahead of me in school, but we were both in the orchestra and marching band. It was truly a God-thing that, 15 years later, they were still part of my life. Through our connection in the church orchestra, I knew them when they got married and started their family. After Jason's and my first daughter, Jordan, was born in January 2003, we sent out birth announcements, including to Cindy and Scott.
>
> One Sunday morning at church, Scott made a comment in passing that Cindy was in the planning stages of starting a business and was looking for a graphic designer. After seeing our nicely designed birth announcements, Scott asked if I was interested. I told him that Jason was the talent behind the announcement. I suggested Cindy and Jason meet at our house to discuss what she was looking for. Jason said yes to the meeting, but he wasn't sure what he was agreeing to. Neither of us were. Little did we realize how much this meeting would change the future for all of us.
>
> The meeting didn't go at all as I expected. I was only there to hear Cindy's proposal and support Jason in whatever he would consider doing to help her. Cindy shared her vision, and Jason was very capable of assisting her on the creative side. But it was clear there were still a lot of details to be managed, and I had the skills

and experience to manage them. My full-time job at the time was as a project traffic coordinator at an advertising agency, so I was well versed in communicating daily details between account executives and graphic designers. Jason suggested that he would help Cindy with a catalog at no expense if she would consider me as a business partner.

My first thought was "I don't have time for this!" I had a new baby to consider, and I really enjoyed my job. But Cindy's vision for the business was intriguing. Since I didn't know what I wanted to do with my life over the long term, this opportunity sounded good in the short term. So, Cindy and I agreed to a partnership with a handshake.

We jumped right in and started planning the first Thirty-One catalog. We featured products Cindy found at AmericasMart Atlanta, a wholesale shopping showroom, and used the vendor-supplied photos. After a few months of development, we had a small quantity of inventory stocked, shipping supplies purchased, and workspaces set up in Cindy's Soddy Daisy basement for our October 1st catalog launch.

At that point in my life, I had had a bit of experience doing direct sales on the side for a kitchenware company prior to working my full-time Insurance job. And I was pretty dang good at it. I knew the best way to begin was to follow that spark buried deep inside me, and the fastest way to fan it into a flame was to let it catch fire with those closest to me first. I had an exciting idea and hoped it would make life better for me, Scott, and the kids. But I really wanted my idea to make life better for other people too—for Julie and Jason and their crew and other women we knew and their families.

Julie and I gathered family and friends at Ryan's Steakhouse to present our plan. The No. 1 question we were asked (and still hear today) was "Why the name Thirty-One?" This gives us the opportunity to talk about what an empowered woman looks like from the biblical description in the Old Testament Book of Proverbs, Chapter

31. The passage describes a virtuous woman who was family-focused, community-oriented, and business-minded. She was known as the landowner who continually prayed for all that she did. According to the passage, this hard-working woman made a difference in the world, and because of her diligence and success at fulfilling her purpose, she was worthy of being celebrated. I saw so many women, including myself, wearing so many different hats and working hard for their families. I wanted us to be recognized, truly seen, and celebrated, just like the woman in Proverbs 31. That's why we've always prioritized *fun* and *celebration.*

My sister, Christie, was a huge support during those early days of turning my vision into reality. I called her our Prayer Warrior. It was a conversation with her that inspired the idea for the name, Thirty-One. I told her how I wanted this business to empower women to be like the woman I read about in Proverbs 31 of the Bible, and how I didn't want the business to carry my own name. Christie said, "Well, Cindy, how about calling your business Thirty-One?" Right away I knew in my gut that's what it had to be. If a name with numbers could work for a jewelry company (1928©), it could work for us too. The name was not only symbolic of the women I wanted to empower, but also a vision of the women we wanted to become. Through Thirty-One, we were reminding women of who they *already* were and who they had the potential to become as they lived a life of purpose and what my Christian community referred to as their *calling.*

In October, Julie and I showed up at the Signal Mountain Hodgepodge Fair in Chattanooga, Tennessee, with 500 copies of our debut catalog and a sampling of our product line. We were still working our full-time jobs, taking care of our families, and supporting our husbands in their work, but that weekend, we began hosting parties on our own and with friends. We shared our gifts and our thirty-one®

Strength & dignity
ARE HER CLOTHING,

and she laughs
AT THE TIME TO COME.

She opens her mouth
WITH WISDOM,

and the teaching
of kindness
IS ON HER TONGUE.

Proverbs 31

business ideas every chance we got in our small-town community. By Christmas, we had more orders than we could handle, plus we landed our first Consultant. Some people may have considered us crazy, but we knew it was more than that. We had a solid business plan, friends who believed in us, and faith that could move mountains . . . mountains of gift orders from my basement out into the world.

2

FAITH

Have Guts

EARLY ON, I would hear myself telling people that my three reasons for getting out of bed and doing what I do every day were *faith, family,* and Thirty-One. I found my faith at an early age, thanks to my mom's commitment to a church community and my grandmother's consistent presence in our lives. We were religious and Southern enough that there was no alcohol or cussing in our home. But we did have playing cards and were allowed to dance, which my mom was not allowed to do growing up.

Mom hit a few rough patches after she and Dad got divorced. But she always loved us, cared for us, and had a steady paying job. At some point, she thought the responsible thing to do was to make sure we attended church. She took my sister and me there every Sunday and most Wednesday nights. We never missed summer vacation Bible school, and Mom even stayed for the adult classes at the same time. I took comfort knowing she didn't drop us off for free babysitting; she was just down the hall learning about Jesus too.

My dad moved back to town while I was still in elementary school. I was delighted to live close again, and my time with Daddy also meant time with his mother, Mamaw. She loved Jesus, reading, and cigarettes. Whenever we spent the night at her house, she let me sleep snuggled up next to her. Her bedroom was just big enough for her bed, a dresser, and the stacks of books she had in every corner. Her walls were yellow from her smoking, but I noticed only how cozy it felt to be wrapped in a blanket lying next to her. Mamaw was also the reason we loved disco music on the eight-track player and watched *Saturday Night Fever*.

My faith was formed between Mamaw's yellow walls and the two places we called home—one with Mom and one with Dad. Jesus was my friend, and God always seemed real. Dad found faith in other ways outside the four walls of a church. But Mamaw was committed to going to Central Baptist Church every Sunday and stopping on the way home to pick up her next pack of cigarettes at the convenience store. On days we rode with Mamaw, she let us pick out our favorite candy bar at the store. Mine was Snickers. Mamaw was the reason my mom began taking us to Central Baptist.

Later, Central Baptist Church in Hixson, Tennessee, was where I married Scott and where he served as the Associate Worship Pastor for a season. It was also where we spent a lot of time as a young family. Being married to a pastor meant the work of ministry was never done, with plenty for every available hand to do. I can't tell you how many hours I volunteered or showed up to support Scott, young kids in tow. For some pastors and their families, this kind of commitment (and, at times, *over*commitment) can lead to a loss of faith. But we were fortunate to realize our faith could be found and forged outside of traditional ministry. For us, faith was included in family outings on the lake in my dad's boat and in our walks in the woods. It was in our generosity as we gave above and beyond our meager means. It was expressed in the love we shared with one another and the way we worshiped God. Faith has often been described as "believing without seeing" and that's exactly what it is for us. We've been fortunate that our beliefs have been reinforced through faith-filled experiences in which we've actually *seen* God come through in big ways in our lives and those of others.

That's not to say my faith hasn't been tested over the years. Loss, betrayal, entitlement, poor timing, bad business decisions, growing family needs, sustainability concerns . . . all of these and more have tested my faith. The inspiration I cling to in these moments is that God has a purpose for me and that is to *love others.*

Julie explains it this way:

> We found success early because we weren't afraid to try and fail. We reminded ourselves time and again that our chances for success were high because we were so dedicated to what we were doing. We saw the times we did fail as lessons and became good at problem-solving. We were in our twenties when we dove into the deep water of the direct sales community. We were blessed with the connections we made in the industry, as most folks were much older and more experienced than us. There's something unique about being young and naïve when you start a business. You have no preconceived notions of what is possible—or impossible.

Facing our fears of failure required more than courage. It demanded the faith to do big things. We had to move to bigger buildings with more space than we needed, and assume titles and roles beyond anything we had done before. This kind of faith—the kind that moves mountains—made it possible for me to have hope, and it enabled me to focus when the work got harder.

One of the most difficult things for a young entrepreneur is believing in herself. I quickly believed in others and in our products, the parties, and the Thirty-One business opportunities. But believing in myself was more difficult because I considered myself "average," based on the standards of school tests, bank accounts, and real-world experience. There were not many female leaders under thirty for me to look up to, and few people expressed confidence in my business abilities or my "little bag gig." In the early days, my biggest fans were Scott and Julie, and I don't know that I could have pushed through without them.

As a young entrepreneur, I struggled with managing the bank account, investing in products, and dealing with overhead and sales commissions, which were our biggest expense. Several times, Julie and I had to muster the courage to ask our parents for loans—and not just small ones. These were desperate requests for $20,000 to $40,000 at a time. The banks were not willing to give us small business loans at the time, and today, I am thankful for how much our parents believed in us. We worked hard to pay off those loans as quickly as possible and were so proud of ourselves when we did. The final payments were confidence boosters, for sure! I appreciate the in-kind faith that has been extended to me, and I pay it forward by helping others to grow their faith and pass it on as well.

3

FOCUS

Work Hard

FOCUS NEVER CAME EASY TO ME. As a kid at school, I'd stare out the window rather than pay attention in my classes. Every time I played in the outfield of a softball game, there was a legitimate risk of me getting hit in the head by fly balls I didn't notice coming my way. Tests indicated I had issues with reading comprehension and ADHD, but back then it was simply ADD: Attention Deficit Disorder. I was fortunate when my mom found a program for kids with ADD. I received help with my inability to sit still and was allowed extra time to take tests. I eventually won a scholarship designated for children with ADD that paid for my college education.

By then, I had learned enough about success to realize that it required focus, and I was determined to do whatever it took to find my own way. I had a good role model: my mom. After my parents' split, I watched her work full-time and take care of the household and our family's needs. She didn't graduate from college, but she received training and certification to do echocardiograms (scanned pictures of the heart) at the local hospital. Because of her example and the respect I had for her and my sister, I earned a degree in marketing from the University of Tennessee–Chattanooga (UTC).

Something else that won my attention during my teenage years was Scott Monroe. We met on July 4, 1990, during the annual Independence Day concert at our church. My sister and I played French horn in the Central Baptist Church orchestra. For special events, our director hired a few experienced musicians to play with us. Scott, a saxophonist, was one of those brought in for this concert. In an orchestra stage layout, the saxophone and French horn sections are adjacent to one another, which meant Scott and I sat side by side for rehearsals and the concert.

As a drum major and upperclassman at UTC, Scott Monroe was a *big deal,* and the July heat worked its magic on us in more ways than one. He asked me out at the concert, not realizing I was only fifteen and still in high school. Scott was seven years older than me (and still is, as I sometimes like to remind him). We ran into each other a few more times throughout marching band season and had our first date five months later, after a Christmas concert on campus where he was playing his saxophone. From that day forward, Scott never dated anyone else, although he had plenty of opportunities. The year I turned 19, we were married at Central Baptist Church, where Mamaw and Mom planted those early seeds of faith. Scott was a worship pastor and touring musician at the time, and I was a full-time student. Daddy was concerned I would drop out of college after I got married, but the mere mention of his fear that I would quit was enough to push me to finish. I saw it as a challenge.

While in college I also got my first dip into direct sales. I needed to make some money but couldn't get a full-time job and still maintain decent grades. Notice, I said "decent grades" because nobody here was making A's. I began selling kitchenware from a catalog and at-home parties. Much to my surprise, I quickly earned the extra incentives too. It was exactly what I needed to balance earning a living while earning my degree.

Eventually, Scott was offered a pastoral staff position at Central Baptist Church. He was living out his calling with lots of purpose and passion but was still making a meager salary, which in those days seemed like pennies. I had a full-time job at an insurance company doing claims and product development. I was able to rub shoulders with a couple of the VPs of our company, and it gave me a wide perspective and big ideas around business planning and management. At 24, I gave birth to our daughter, Alyx, but continued to work full-time.

We sold our starter home and bought a plot of land to create our own hand-built house. We lived in a 35-foot pull-behind camper near our land while we built the house because it was the only way we could afford to make it happen. Talk about dreamers—that was *us*! Scott loves to tell about the day we worked on the house well after dark, using our car's headlights so we could see. I was up on a ladder, seven months pregnant, hammering vinyl siding. Those days shaped the rest of our lives. Our son, Evan, was born two and a half years after Alyx, and with his arrival, we knew our family was complete.

We moved into the home we hand-built in Soddy Daisy, Tennessee, a 23 square-mile suburb on the northeastern side of Chattanooga with a population of around 13,000. This is where we established roots, developed friendships, and raised our kids. At the end of 2003, it also was where, with faith and focus, Thirty-One was blossoming into a full-time business from our basement.

In November that year, we added our first Consultant, Jenny Hillenburg, and our first party host, Dawn Brown. We got past our first fall catalog and the Christmas season. At the start of 2004, we were six months in and onto the spring catalog season. Julie and I were still working our full-time jobs, as we tested gifts, such as citronella candles shaped like croquette balls, grilling and gardening tools, and even a bug-zapper. By late summer, we had made enough money to pay Cathy Smith, our dear friend and fellow "Founding Mother" (as we affectionately call ourselves), to be all things for all people. Cathy's love for people, can-do spirit, and attention to detail were the glue we needed to hold together the strategy and sales at our end. Cathy started taking care of office-management needs: billing, bookkeeping, answering phones, packing orders, and making deliveries to Consultants and customers. Her priority was keeping everyone happy and productive so the business could thrive. It was no easy task during those early months of building teams.

In our first Thirty-One product catalog, our collection included purses shaped like ceramic cookie jars or made from collegiate license plates, stationery, candles, bags, and totes. Julie remembers some early products:

> We didn't realize how hard it would be to convince customers to shop for food from a gift catalog. Our second catalog trial and error was a food line including prepackaged soup mixes and biscuit makings, as well as pies and other desserts. We did a taste test with four or five local Consultants at one of our monthly meetings, and they caught us off guard when they said they didn't like the soup we served them, not knowing it was a product we were adding to the upcoming catalog line.

Three simple items became our biggest hits: bags, purses, and totes. A thermal tote and a large utility tote in fun colors stole the show. We made the crucial decision to offer monogramming on these soft-good items. Our first catalog had only one item that could be embroidered, but that choice led to many more items that sold well because they were personalized. That's when we really started to grow. By our fourth and fifth catalogs in the spring and fall of 2005, we were mostly selling thermal totes and bags with the option for monogramming. We still had a lot to learn about product development and design, but we were fiery and focused.

In early 2004, Julie was laid off from her marketing job with three months of unemployment. This bought us the time we needed to get further down the road. I went from thinking I could start a business and just see where it went to realizing this was a BIG deal and needed more of my time. The insurance company where I was generously employed saw the tension I was feeling from juggling both jobs, and we came to an agreement for me to go part-time. The back-and-forth between two jobs lasted six more months before I finally stepped down to give all my attention to Thirty-One.

My new goal was for us to make it to five years. I had read in business books that eighty-five percent of start-up businesses didn't make it past five years. This sounded like a challenge, and by then we all knew what happened when I was challenged. But it wasn't just me—or even me, Julie, and Cathy—who had to rise to the challenge so our little business could survive. Our families would have to take the ride with us.

4

FAMILY

Love Your People

WE NEVER WOULD HAVE GOTTEN as far as we did if it hadn't been for the love and support of our families. I know a lot of people say that when they want to give credit after finding success. But for us, the way our families contributed to our success truly made all the difference. For starters, I didn't have to wait in a long line to enroll my kids in daycare because Scott's mom, Beverly Monroe, was always there. When Alyx was a baby, Beverly would hold her sweet little face and slowly sound out the word "G-rand-moth-er." But all Alyx could repeat back was "G-er." So, it stuck, not just for Alyx but for all of us. Ger was our rock. She took care of our kids and Scott's ailing dad, who had lung cancer on top of Parkinson's disease. When PaPa Jack passed away, Ger stepped in to support us in every possible way. On the rare occasion when Ger needed a break, my stepmom, Carol, was there. We also had many dinners at Dad and Carol's, and Carol helped me with our never-ending pile of laundry. My mom was working full-time but provided Sunday lunch, weekend help, and more. Later on, Ger moved with us several states away from her home in Chattanooga to support our crazy dream. She is known and loved by all of the Consultants who attend our annual conferences. Even now, as she turns 90, Ger is the kindest, most caring woman I know, and someone I want to be like when I grow up.

Our support came from more than just our parents. We had our sisters, brothers, cousins, and, of course, our husbands and kids. For Christmas 2004, we missed the cutoff date for shipping at our local UPS store. So our husbands, Jason, and Scott, hand-delivered the remaining orders. Thank goodness our sales were still mostly local that year, and the guys delivered the orders in a day or two. I wish I could say we never missed another UPS shipping deadline again, but we were always working up to the last minute in those days.

As our business grew, monogrammed thermal and utility totes were still our hottest items, and the monogramming meant *we* were the ones who had to do the sewing. We bought two monogramming machines and taught ourselves how to use them. Cathy, Julie, and I would take turns sewing, filling orders, and packing boxes to ship—until the day Julie put a machine needle through her finger. We decided her skills were better used in creating the systems and processes we desperately needed. Cathy took over on the sewing and became the monogramming queen.

One of our machines broke in the middle of another big sales season. Our production immediately went down thirty percent. Scott came to the rescue. After taking the whole machine apart and trying to fix it himself, realizing time was money, Scott drove the machine to the factory where it was made in Memphis—five hours away. That was like taking our Honda straight to the factory headquarters to get it fixed and skipping the dealership. It took a lot of nerve for Scott to do what he did to get our machine fixed before the holidays, but those were the kinds of decisions our family members made out of love for us.

To keep up with demand, we outsourced some monogramming

to a lady a couple towns over. We would haul our products in large black trash bags to meet our monogrammer halfway alongside the road. But we still couldn't keep up, and we had to make even bigger decisions on how to keep under one roof everything we did: inventory storage, monogramming, and shipping.

As sales grew, so did our days. We'd make promises to our families to be home in time to help with dinner, but our husbands knew that was code for "I'll be home to help set the table before heading back to the basement to work again." Soon the guys would take turns bringing us meals in the warehouse (chili nights were amazing!). The kids would help us or hang out and play together until they were tucked into a Pack 'n' Play or snuggled up in blankets on a mat. Those were the days of "warehouse walls" built by the kids with our boxes of inventory and ants invading our space to consume the Goldfish snacks they left behind. Our families made more sacrifices of love in those days than we'll ever really know.

From Julie's perspective:

> We wouldn't have been able to invest the time and energy into Thirty-One without the support of our families. My husband, Jason, worked hard to support our family in the early years when we couldn't pay ourselves much from the Thirty-One revenue. All of us reinvested into the business to the detriment of our own bank accounts. My parents and in-laws were super supportive with helping to watch our daughter, Jordan, while Jason and I both worked way beyond a normal 40-hour workweek.
>
> Having our kids with us while we worked in the basement or, eventually, in the warehouse wasn't a pretty sight. But you can't overstate the impact on these children from witnessing their moms working so hard on something they believed in with all their hearts.
>
> Our founding employees became like family since we spent so much time together. We built lifetime bonds. Our children grew close

and even acted like siblings at times. My family made all the hard work worthwhile, and their support was invaluable.

We made sacrifices for them too. In 2004, we moved the business out of my basement into our first building. The guys were there to build racks, set up displays, and fix whatever needed fixin'. But we knew we couldn't just keep *taking* from our loved ones; we also had to *give*. With our feet a little more grounded in our growing business, we established weekly family dinners. We'd stop work by 5:30 p.m. every Wednesday to meet with our families at Cracker Barrel and have dinner together. Six adults and five kids made for some memorable impromptu gatherings. Cathy's kids, Savannah and Dakota, were the oldest; my kids, Alyx and Evan, were in the middle; and Julie's daughter, Jordan, was the youngest.

Before long there were more than just three of us on the team. We had six original "Founding Mothers": me, Julie, Cathy, Julie's sister Laura, Erin, and Kim. We saw ourselves as the *Golden Girls* or perhaps more celebrity-relevant at the time, *Charlie's Angels*—except that we didn't need a Charlie! This was the start of our sisterhood, backed by our dedicated and supportive husbands and thirteen kids (with more to come). As our Thirty-One crew grew, we treated them like family too.

We each had important roles, but always knew we might need to put on a different hat at any moment. I was over product development, strategy, the sales field, and worked with Scott on marketing and communications. Julie was our project manager, inventory buyer, sales forecaster, information-technology systems owner, and she held our strategy document together as processes evolved. Along with bookkeeping, Cathy took over monogramming and backorders operations, then product development and quality control, then our recognition department, and wound up working in our sales department to welcome new Consultants. Laura basically owned everything that fell under shipping and receiving. Kim ran our customer service department. And Erin helped with a little bit of everything from making bracelets to monogramming to shipping, sales field support, career and guideline support, and our recognition department. We were all committed to wearing as many hats as it took for us to make the business successful. That was part of what we stood for: celebrating women for all the hats we wear as children, moms, wives, friends, entrepreneurs, employees, and more.

We worked hard and loved one another. We took time to pause together in whatever ways we could. In our second year of business, Cathy started our first annual Thanksgiving dinner with everyone signing up to bring a dish. On Thanksgiving Day, we brought our food, covered our worktables with brown paper, and sat down for a meal together. Those were ways we made special memories amid those hectic moments.

Growing as fast as we did was exciting, but growth also brought its own challenges. One was maintaining the culture we built from the beginning. Establishing a family culture was part of who we were and how we lived our lives outside the business. We had to fight hard to protect that culture as we grew so fast. Many seasoned professionals in human resources and corporate management would caution a company like ours not to become too friendly on a personal level with all the staff. They say things like "Friends are friends. Business is business." That makes sense, I guess, but it also felt like a way to rationalize not caring about the well-being of teammates, or even mistreating them. Because we built the entire business with close friends who shared similar Christian values and came from loving families, it was important for us to reflect those values in our business, no matter how fast we grew or how big we got.

That doesn't mean it wasn't difficult at times. One of the most painful things I've ever had to do was tell a dear friend she could no longer work for us. I lost sleep after a reorganization meant we had to let some people go. Those decisions are painful to think about to this day. But when I step back and look at the big picture, I'll never regret doing our best to build a business and maintain a family-centered culture at Thirty-One.

We added many Consultants as our sales grew at an incredibly fast pace. We went from one Consultant in 2003, to twenty at the end of 2004, to fifty in 2005, and two hundred and fifty in 2006. Our Consultant numbers and sales figures skyrocketed from there. We grew so fast, we became concerned that if we didn't pause to document and define our culture, it might disappear. We realized from our prior professional experiences that if a company's culture isn't documented, it starts to take a new shape every time someone else joins the team, bringing their previous experiences with them. We took time as an Executive Team to talk through what our mission, vision, and values were. These definitions were already ingrained in us, so we weren't trying to recreate them. They were the way we lived and loved each other well. But we needed a framework around them so we could share them with newcomers in a clear and consistent way. Defining our vision, mission, and values also served as a way for us to hold each other accountable to them. We worked hard and loved hard in those early days. But we knew it was time to keep expanding the invitation for more people to join us on our journey. We kept making the ask.

FOUNDING TEAM STORY: Cathy Smith

I met Cindy and Julie in 2004 through my new friend, Jenny Hillenburg. Jenny and her husband had recently started attending our church, and we struck up a friendship after their first Sunday at

Central Baptist. Later, we joined a small group with the Hillenburgs, the Suttons, the Monroes, and a few others. I remember Cindy and Jenny sitting at the kitchen table one evening talking about something called Thirty-One, so I asked, "What is Thirty-One?"

Jenny and I were hanging out at the park with our kids a few weeks later and were talking about Thirty-One. I told her to let me know if there was ever a time Cindy needed help in the office. A few days later, Cindy called and asked if I would be interested in helping her and Julie with the business. We met at McDonald's the next morning after dropping our children off at school. I was hired on the spot and started working the next day.

On August 22, 2004, I reported to Cindy's home, where I began working with her and Julie in the basement as the secretary and bookkeeper. Soon my responsibilities grew into packaging and delivering orders, frequent trips to UPS and the post office, and making bracelets. Eventually, Cindy bought our first PR600 Monogram machine and trained me to monogram totes and bags.

What we affectionately refer to as our "basement days" were filled with work downstairs, phone calls outside in search of cell service, and lunches in Cindy's kitchen with our kids during school breaks and summer vacations. But at least those early days smelled lovely. We sold candles in our first few catalogs, and the orders lined the hallway from the garage to our basement office area.

I also remember the day a UPS driver dropped off some of our products and asked, "What is this? One of those basement businesses?" Then he said, "It will probably never make it." Oh, how I wish I would have gotten his name!

This is how it all started!

5

COURAGE

Make the Ask

I KNEW FROM THE BEGINNING that the direct sales model worked. I had my own successful experience selling cataloged kitchenware through direct sales in college, and I was certain this would be the way forward for our little company. Julie and Cathy also had previous experience with this business model, so they bought into direct sales from the beginning. In my mind, it was the best way to keep our overhead costs low. But more than that, it was a good way to earn extra income and an even better way to empower women. For us, the product was just the means; our friendships were the way to our end, which was building a viable business. All we had to do was find the courage to *make the ask.*

Most people assume "the ask" made in a direct sales company goes something like this: "Join our company, purchase products from yourself, and you can earn a full-time income." But that's an *old* multi-level-marketing (MLM) kind of ask and not what we were about at Thirty-One. Our ask sounded more like this: "Would you like to build your own business, make some extra cash, sell amazing products, and empower other women to do the same?" *Do you hear the difference?* The old way held a stigma that promotes a consumer mentality and often "feels slimy" to people on the receiving end of the ask. That model has too often been about self-consuming the products and recruiting others to mostly benefit a few people at the top of the hierarchy. But direct selling—what we referred to as a "party plan" or a more current version of multi-level marketing—is creating a business to sell products to customers. If those customers seem like they could benefit from an opportunity to do the same, the Consultant encourages them to start their own business. These new Consultants then find their own customers and build their own team.

Part of what we liked about the party-plan model came from our belief in the transformational importance of community—gathering women together—not just the transactional exchange of business. We placed great value on connecting with others in a fun environment, and we always believed we could leverage our product and business model to improve relational connections. On the networking side, relationships were an invaluable tool to building and growing our business. For many of our Consultants, it has worked both ways: They grow their businesses while growing their relationships. We believe that what set us apart from other direct sales companies is that we placed more emphasis on stronger, deeper relationships as our desired outcome. This was part of our mission.

We also weren't afraid to call out our Consultants if they were using their relationships *only* to sell products. We often had a "Don't Be Weird" talk with them as a way to protect our mission, our brand, and their own personal brands. "Please don't be THAT lady, bless her heart," we'd say. We never wanted our Consultants to come across as obnoxious or pushy or have anyone avoid them in the grocery store. Yes, our Consultants are passionate about products, parties, and their businesses, but that passion comes through best when they are genuinely focused on others, and not merely on a new order of bags. We regularly remind them that we were more about *serving* than *selling*, or as one of our employees once put it, "We're more of a cause than a business." It helped that our products provided valuable and specific solutions for the everyday lives of busy women—professionals, creatives, educators, moms, business owners, and travelers. We could help women solve problems and find solutions for their messy, busy, chaotic seasons and corners of life. With this solid, replicable party-plan business model and our amazing products, all we had to do was *make the ask*.

We began looking for great people to host Thirty-One parties. I thought that once we could share about our products and vision, the hostesses would see how easy and fun it was to be a Consultant and want to join our team. My first ask was in the fall of 2003 to Dawn Brown. It wasn't a good time for her, but she became my first hostess and later joined Thirty-One. My second ask was to Jenny Hillenburg, a friend from church who was a stay-at-home mom with three kids. She lived in a fabulous suburban neighborhood where many product parties were already happening. Jenny agreed to host a party and was a big supporter when we rolled out that first catalog. We thought she would make the perfect first Thirty-One Consultant. She started right away building a team, and her business took off.

Consultants wanted to join our team for various reasons. Some joined so they never had to pay full price for our products once they discovered the helpful solutions those items added to their lives. Others joined to earn extra income to help pay for such expenses as vacations, home maintenance projects, and private school tuition. Plus, our Consultants had the flexibility to work when and how often they wanted to work and the option of building their businesses online, in-person, or both. We continue to expand this flexibility for our Thirty-One Consultants.

Leaving the house to build a business is optional today. Many of our hostesses, also known as "insiders," love to invite friends over for wine night, to show off new updates to their houses, or to watch the season kick-off of their favorite TV show. Humans need community and love to gather together. That's why I believe there will always be a place for in-person parties to sell our products and invite others to join our team. Being in-person enables the building of relationships that can't be replicated online or through social media.

While we love in-person parties whenever possible, more than eighty percent of our Consultants run their businesses from their cars, on ballfields, or through social media platforms. Consultants can follow up with customers and build relationships with insiders and hosts through text-messaging platforms. That's why building a company brand was so crucial from the beginning. We knew our reputable collective brand was vital to helping Consultants build their personal brands. Our bottom line was that we offered life solutions to help families. We recognized that the customers and Consultants we most often attracted were busy moms who wanted discounts, extra income, and community. These were women who loved their people and wanted a fresh way to build new relationships. That's why they loved Thirty-One.

Later in 2005, Julie and I were both in the business full-time, and Cathy was with us as much as she could be. We got our first company conference under our belts with about thirty Consultants in Fort Oglethorpe, Georgia, while we were in the middle of another round of office expansions. I knew I needed a break, so I took time to attend a spiritual retreat where I found rest and a renewed sense of mission. I sensed God asking me to keep running through open doors with the business. I shared this vision with Julie and Cathy, and they were willing to keep running with me. So, that's what we did. And we never ever made an ask we weren't willing to answer ourselves.

We had to make eight moves in our first eight years because of our growth. We just kept making the ask to empower other women and our teams expanded. We had a saying back then: "Welcome to Thirty-One where everything changes every thirty-one minutes!" We started in my basement in Soddy Daisy, then moved to a small office on Middle Valley Road in neighboring Hixson. Next we got an office-warehouse combination on Old Hixson Pike before moving to the Shallowford Road warehouse in Chattanooga. Then we went partially back to Old Hixson Pike because we needed the extra office space, before we eventually moved business operations to another state (more on that in Part Two).

Every time we made the ask to empower more women and expand our team, it required back-end business decisions. We had to take time out of our already packed schedules to connect with experts and advisers and develop a new round of strategies. And it meant a whole lot of prayin' for all of us.

Julie remembers the details of that time so well:

> The building on Middle Valley Road was a sixteen-hundred-square-foot warehouse located in the nearby town of Hixson, still convenient to our homes. We signed a two-year lease with high hopes the bigger space would last us for a while. The new office and operations area was a large open space with no walls and a single bathroom in the corner. Once a video rental store, the warehouse still had the original blue carpet and a video return slot in the door, which made a handy mail drop for us. The front of the building had all-glass walls, which quickly became our enemy with the summer heat. We put up vertical blinds to block the sun and save on our air-conditioning bill.
>
> Mr. T's Pizza was on one side of us and a hair salon on the other side. The pizza joint was the best neighbor for a business like ours. We worked nonstop and frequently fed ourselves and our families off

their menu. They served the best late-night pizza you could imagine and had a large selection of ice cream flavors. They even let us have free refills on soft drinks all day long. We needed all the energy we could find as we grew the business, and their pizza and sweets did the trick.

The hair salon caused issues until they finally moved out, and we expanded into their area for the additional eight hundred-square-foot space. But before they moved, I remember coming into the office one morning only to find soaking-wet carpet everywhere. There was a busted pipe behind the salon sinks and water ran into our space overnight. We spent the whole next day running wet vac and fans instead of getting our actual work done. To make matters worse, there was no support from the landlord, so we had to do the work ourselves to restore the space.

Cindy focused on keeping the business moving forward with product selections for the next catalog, managing the finances, communicating with Consultants, and sewing products on one of the four embroidery machines by then. I was still managing the website, processing commission payouts, handling returns, as well as purchasing inventory, and tracking the data. Cathy was our part-time bookkeeper and monogram shop supervisor. And Laura stocked the inventory as well as processing and shipping out the orders. We were all-hands-on-deck, and we soon needed more help.

The early years were so hectic with Cindy and I both working full-time jobs outside of Thirty-One. The one benefit was that we both worked in downtown Chattanooga, just a few blocks from each other. We'd meet several times a week before or after work for curb-side car conversations to handle Thirty-One business and key communications. No matter what it took, we kept the business moving forward on a day-to-day basis. Working full-time and starting this new business gave us the appreciation of the opportunity we were creating for others who dreamed of not having to work full-time for someone else.

I couldn't have said it any better. That's exactly why we had the confidence to *make the ask*: We were making life better for the women who decided to join us.

And then there were the times when other people made an ask of us. Cathy often reminds us of the day a girl named Brandi walked into our office and asked if we were hiring. We said yes but didn't even have an application for her to complete. We liked our conversation with her, so we hired her on the spot. We hired so fast in those days just to keep up with the demand, but we didn't always have the process ironed out. Cathy stepped in to help us with hiring, so we could make a better ask when inviting others to join our team. We also invited our families to help us fill holiday orders so we could be ready for Christmas. We invited sisters, moms, cousins, aunts, grandmothers, and friends. We weren't afraid to make the ask if it meant we eventually got to take a much-needed holiday break at home.

We also made big asks and giant leaps with full confidence, only to be humbled by a good sense of humor. Like the time our online order forms had an open answer for whether a customer wanted to monogram their bags. If they didn't want the monogram, the instructions were to respond NONE. Well, guess what? Yep! Several hundred bags arrived in homes with the word NONE monogrammed on them. And we will never forget the time we featured a Thirty-One Sand Bucket in our spring catalog, just in time for some summer fun . . . except we sold the bucket *with* the sand—40 pounds of sand, to be exact. You can only imagine what that did to shipping costs at our end. But shipping sand was a novel idea and sounded like a lot of fun at the time. Then there was the batch of thermal tote bags that got all fuzzy after just a few uses—like a sweater gets "pills" after it has been worn. It was embarrassing to see our Consultants and customers carrying around fuzzy-yet-fairly-new thermal totes with our name on them. Still these lunch totes were one of our best-selling items. At another point, we decided to hand-paint some of our inventory. As we developed the product and did quality testing for our fabrics, we concluded it was better to use printed art rather than try hand-painting.

In 2007, Scott Monroe stepped down from his full-time job as a worship pastor to take over marketing and communications. He eventually become our Chief Brand Officer. Most entrepreneurs built their brands and then built their businesses, but we did it the other way around. Again, we desperately needed direction and help to clarify and communicate our *why*. That's where Scott stepped in. His position was less about branding (designing all the marks, logos, and elements a brand is known by) and more about our cultural brand as a company. As Scott likes to say, "Brand is what people say about you when you're not in the room." And if people were going to talk about us when we weren't in the room, we wanted to give them some clear language and a defined brand to talk about.

6

PURPOSE

Define Your Why

EARLY ON, we began saying things like "Our company supports more than the *material* parts of life. It also supports the *emotional* parts of life." We knew that other women wanted to be part of an amazing community and provide for their families. They wanted to be able to help pay for braces and family vacations and reduce their mortgage. They also wanted to help women—family and friends—find the same opportunities. Another of our observations was "Our products help women find new solutions for their busy lives as their kids grow and their lives evolve." These statements were true then and still are today.

We also discovered just how important *style* was to our business and brand. Our Consultants and customers wanted not only solutions; they wanted stylish solutions. Each season, we picked new prints for our bags and totes to meet that goal, giving our customers opportunities to buy again when their style preferences changed and our Consultants new products and solutions to offer. We didn't have just a business brand; we also had an emotional brand. Our business did better the more we told stories of how our products provided solutions and our business model provided community, support, and financial opportunity for our people. There was no mistaking how much our business opportunities were starting to impact whole families and communities. The more defined our *why* became the more we grew.

Cathy would remind us that our success was measured by the way we made people feel, and we were great at that. Our people, not our products, were our *why*. Better products with trend-setting styles helped our people feel more seen, and they empowered them to live out their own *why*.

In 2007, we partnered with a new vendor called Atrium for product sourcing and development. They became our primary go-to for all the stylish products we had to offer. The best part of working with a designated vendor like Atrium was that we now knew where all our products came from. They were coming from soft-goods and sewing factories in central China, also partners of Atrium. Now we weren't just empowering women and making lives better here in the United States. We were empowering and encouraging more than six thousand families around the globe. Scott once told our Consultants, "Because of you, others have the opportunity to succeed and thrive. Even though we're half a world away, we're creating better schools, communities, and families, and because of that, we're creating a better world. Better families make a better world." We were so grateful for that opportunity.

Our partnership with Atrium also allowed us to make products exclusive to Thirty-One. The bags and totes purchased by our customers could be found only through us. Not only did we benefit from our committed partnership with Atrium the company, but we also benefited from individual people. Some of their people became our people as we grew big enough to hire more of an Executive Team. But before we could build out the executive level of our business, we had to do another round of defining our *why*.

I was certain God allowed us to get to this point of growth so we could keep our mission of empowering and encouraging women to figure out their own *why* and realize they had everything they needed to reach for their dreams! This was our overarching vision, and we worked hard to turn it into reality through our company mission:

> *Thirty-One is more than just a company. We are people who believe in celebrating, encouraging, and rewarding others for who they are.*

And we articulated our company vision like this:

> *The Thirty-One vision is to give women many of the tools to help them earn supplemental income, support their personal "whys" and make their goals simple, easy, fun, and full of rewarding experiences.*

This mission and vision would evolve and take on new language over time, and eventually, it would include a set of values that became the pillars of everything we did. This was the best way we knew how to define our *why*, which translated into encouraging, empowering, and providing solutions for the modern-day woman and rewarding those who became Consultants with great benefits. This vision, mission, and values were our compass and guide for the decisions we made daily at work and in our personal lives. They were our personal *why*.

Establishing our *why* became important to us after we read a book by Simon Sinek titled *Start with Why*. I highly recommend it. We discovered in reading his book that, without a strong *why*, people won't be motivated to stay connected to a brand, a product, or an organization. Sinek introduced us to the idea that, while our overall purpose as a business can remain consistent, an individual's personal *why* can change over time. And here's how this played out for us at Thirty-One. Many of our Consultants would tell us their original *why* for joining our team was more about needing extra cash or getting out of the house for a change of scenery. Over time, however, these women would tell us that their *why* became more intrinsic. Their personal *why* now included internal desires to belong to a sisterhood of community, to become a more confident person, to collaborate and share their joys and successes with other women as colleagues and friends. For some, building their business even became about growing in their relationship with God. Part of my personal *why* was always to give women choices. Seeing our Consultants make choices that led to real-life change was one of the greatest fulfillments of my purpose. We had to make sure the *why* of our business left space for the ever-evolving *why* of our Consultants because, at the end of the day, *they were our business.*

And here's what I learned about myself in the process of building a business with a strong *why*. When my work life was aligned with my personal *why*, I had more energy to live out my purpose by serving and leading others. But when I doubted my purpose or wasn't focused on living out my personal *why*, I got drained of energy and found myself feeling cranky or depressed. That's when I knew it was time to reach out to a personal coach, a peer group, my husband Scott, or really close friends I trusted. I've also gone on group retreats, personal retreats, and participated in coaching calls and counseling to support that strong desire I had to be living and working in my purpose. Thirty-One has allowed me to not only live out my *why*, but it's also given me numerous opportunities to share about the importance of finding your own *why*, also referred to as your calling or purpose. Whatever resonated with the women we were serving in our business, we wanted them to find it. But we also had to model it as a company and as leaders.

Scott would remind me that acknowledging how our personal *why* affected our company *why* wasn't selfish. It was about taking care of ourselves so we could take care of others. He said it was less "What's in it for me?" and more "What's in me for it?" This meant discovering what we personally have to bring to the business, brand, and community. Showing up with a strong sense of purpose and *why* is what allowed us to have such a great impact, not just in the lives of our Consultants, but also in the communities where they lived out their own strong sense of purpose and *why*. This kind of impact just kept on giving as it spilled over to our company, our Consultants, our hosts and customers, their local communities, and even to our vendors and their teams.

Here's how Julie defined her *why* back then:

> My "why" was always about my family. I worked hard to provide the best life for my children and model for them the results of hard work. I didn't start my journey in Thirty-One with the goal of growing a business to a certain revenue amount or growing our Consultant count to a certain number. I started because I felt led to bring to life Cindy's vision of empowering and encouraging other women with an opportunity that could change their lives in big and small ways.
>
> One of the most asked questions we hear about the start of Thirty-One is "Did you ever expect the business to grow like it did?" Our answer was always the same: NO! We never expected it, nor would we have wanted to know how large the company would grow. Understanding WHY we were working so hard was what kept us focused on the mission of improving women's lives. I truly believe that had I known from the beginning that we would grow like lightning and in six short years move out of state, I would have run the other way. Tennessee was our home, and Jason and I never imagined we would ever leave.

Our collective *why* was rooted in our deep faith in God and the Bible as God's Word. The two verses that lit a fire in my belly and helped me stay focused in my mind were: "He who began a good work in you is faithful to completion" (Philippians 1:6), and "I can do all things through Christ who strengthens me" (Philippians 4:13). We truly believed God was strengthening us in ways only God could do as we encouraged our Consultants to find their *why* and empowered them to live out their purpose and calling—all because of the good and hard work we were doing at Thirty-One.

Remember those values we were working on earlier? As our *why* became increasingly clear as a company, so did our values. Eventually, we narrowed down the list and came up with twelve values that still stand as pillars of our business today:

Purposeful
Passionate
Authentic
Thankful
Courageous
Flexible
Respectful
Hard-working
Generous
Curious
Fun-loving
Accountable

These values represented what it meant for us to live out our *why* at Thirty-One. In Chapter 30, we will get to how we defined each one of these values. But for now, these are the values that became the guiding principles of our purpose and our *why*.

7

PASSION

Be All In

THERE IS ONLY ONE WAY to "be" at Thirty-One, and that is to be *all in*. Don't get me wrong, Consultants aren't asked to make this their full-time job. There have always been Consultants who are "hobbyists'' and do this mostly for fun. Many women sell our products part-time to supplement a full-time job, contribute more to their household income, and build a little vacation fund or a goal-oriented account for extras like Christmas, sports sign-ups, and music lessons.

There are women who do make this their full-time career. They are the CEOs of their own small businesses. We call these women "micro-entrepreneurs." Whichever way these women, and even a few men, chose to engage with us, one thing was certain: They went *all in*. We modeled this way of being from the inside out. We believe the Bible when it said to "Do whatever you do as though you're doing it for the Lord" (1 Corinthians 10:31). Our Thirty-One family is full of people who did just that. Their dedication to their faith was the inspiration for truly being *all in*.

The best example of how it looked for our team to be *all in* was Laura Smith. Laura was one of our six "Founding Mothers." She is Julie's older sister, and we're all quick to say she was the hardest working person our company had in the early days, and possibly *ever*. Laura had the strength and endurance of a machine. Whatever we asked her to do, she would dive right in. Not only did she act fast, but she also did good work. She was the first to move and build racks and take care of the huge piles of boxing and shipping. She was also a fast learner on the monogramming machine. Plus, Laura was the first employee who was certified to run a forklift. Our new warehouse came with one, and we needed an operator. We didn't realize just what Laura's forklift license would unleash in her until she unloaded the first tractor-trailer load of inventory like a *boss*. She ran our warehouse operations masterfully and never complained about the lack of air conditioning behind the hottest seat in the house. And when our product racks didn't fit in one of our office buildings, she was with Julie and me when we took sawzalls to the racks to make them fit. Whatever Laura did for the company, she was *all in*.

Julie was right up there with Laura. She took a "weekend maternity leave" when her son was born in 2006. As soon as sweet Jacob was in her arms, she was already thinking about the next steps necessary at work. Laura and Julie were quiet, strategic, steady, and committed. And they taught the rest of us what it means to be loyal.

When it comes to passion, Cathy is the one who led this charge. No matter her title, which changed often over sixteen years, she was the first to notice when something wasn't going well with team members. She was also the last one standing with them, making sure they had whatever was needed to work through the problem. She was the heart and soul of our home team.

We were always dreaming up new ideas to smooth the way for employees and Consultants joining our team so they could jump in with both feet from the start. We came up with an enrollment kit for new Consultants that contained essentials to make it easier for them to sell products, build a team, and empower their peers to do the same. Initially, the kit shipped in a plain brown cardboard box, but as soon as we could make it happen, we packed them in signature pink boxes, making them impossible to miss on delivery. New Consultants also received our best-selling products, amazing training materials, and constant support. Our goal was for every new Consultant to find success quickly so she could earn back her starter-kit investment and reach her financial goals. Ultimately, this investment and support is what helped our Consultants develop and live out their *why*.

Another way we bolstered our Consultants so they could be *all in* was with the annual conference. Two years into our business, we decided a conference sounded like fun and seemed like the best way to bring everyone together for a few days of encouragement, laughter, strategy, empowerment, and new product reveal. Our conferences became the highlight of every sales year.

Conference time was always a high point for me, but it took a lot of energy. Leading up to the conference was a stressful time. I had to write a few talks, including a closing talk with Scott, which in my mind carried the most weight. We had rehearsals, products to prep, and all of the details that go into pulling off a big event. We maximized our time by making each conference a Thirty-One family affair. We believe that our behaviors are caught more than taught, so we always had our kids around. We didn't want them to only hear about the work we did. We wanted them to see it and participate with us. They each had a role: Evan would hand out Consultant awards, looking so cute in his suit. Alyx modeled products for our fall catalog reveals. And Julie's son, Jacob, bolstered our shipping update dressed in a brown UPS suit. Conference times were the best version of all of us being *all in* with the business and with each other.

It's no surprise that many of our Consultants are women of the

Christian faith, although this was definitely not a requirement. With a name and a network like ours from the deep South, we drew a Christian faith-informed crowd. Since I am married to a man who was once a worship pastor and continues to always be a pastor to people no matter where he is, we ended every conference with a morning of worship. Attendance was not expected, and we made clear it was optional. We simply wanted to acknowledge that our way of being *all in* meant giving thanks to God, who makes all things possible. Above all, we hoped our expression of faith translated into a call of action to love for everyone on our team. We always strive to be inclusive of everyone, no matter their faith, cultural heritage, neighborhood, or socio-economic background. We truly believe that LOVE is the truest expression of what it means to be *all in*. The love that exuded from our Consultants became quite the tidal wave as our Consultant numbers multiplied. We grew from 250 Consultants in 2006 to 1,500 in 2007 and 4,000 in 2008. We were becoming a *force* for love and good in the world.

Another way we championed love was the conference talk Scott has given for over a decade to the husbands, partners, and family members of our Consultants. We called it the HOT Class, for Husbands of Thirty-One. The title was a fun and cheeky reference, but everyone who attended our conference in support of a Consultant was welcome, and we were mindful to use inclusive language. This luncheon conversation turned into a full-blown conference session when our Consultants were showing up at conferences feeling frustrated that their husbands "hated their businesses." Scott joked that this session was really undercover marriage advice, which was partly true. Because of his pastor's heart, he was already very good at giving advice.

Scott has always been my biggest fan, and if I am *all in* on something then he is *all in* too. He has supported me in ways that helped the business run smoother and our employees be happier. We showed our Consultants how transparent and authentic we are as a couple and as a company. Scott also helped me celebrate the highs of leadership. He encouraged me to invest our personal money back into the business, and he gave me perspective on how to balance work and family. So, it was fitting for Scott to lead a conference session on how husbands, friends, and family could best support their loved ones who are Consultants. For Scott and me, learning to work together as entrepreneurs and still love one another is one of our greatest accomplishments in life.

Scott had a few key principles he shared consistently with our HOTs community. He always spoke off-the-cuff with no scripted talking points to maintain authenticity and relevance and allow him to read the room. A lot of skeptical partners showed up at annual conferences with their Consultant to see what we were all about. Scott welcomed their skepticism as a fun challenge. He gave the best leadership talks to the most skeptical crowds.

Because those talks are so good, I'll share a few of his points here. They helped our Consultants and their families be *all in* with us. It was important to Scott for the supporting cast around our Consultants to understand first and foremost that our company was not a scam. Thirty-One is a legitimate, profitable business built with the best human intentions and known in the direct sales industry as "a force for good and stability in the world." Our particular industry had long been plagued by a less-than-stellar reputation because of the old multi-level-marketing model many people entered into, only to discover it was next to impossible to actually make money. Many of these HOTs knew people who had been "burned" in some sort of direct sales business or "pyramid scheme." So Scott was always careful to make sure this crew understood that we were not a pyramid scheme (which is illegal) or a "purse cult," as some jokingly called us back in the day. We went above and beyond as a company to set up our Consultants for the best chances of success with a low cost of entry and a competitive compensation plan. Scott told stories of how Julie and I didn't take paychecks for the first few *years* in the business, and how it was never our goal or intention to "get rich." That was the first big hurdle to get over with many of these men and other family supporters.

Scott asked husbands of our team leaders to share their personal stories of what we jokingly referred to as the "Thirty-One Conversion." He knew the conference crowd could relate to them better than to himself as a successful company executive. These guys shared funny and often deeply emotional stories of the positive changes they saw in their wives through the business, as well as specific ways they learned to support their spouses over the years in Thirty-One. Scott reminded the guys that they didn't have to, nor should they, come in and take over their wives' businesses. He would say, "Guys, this is her thing. Let her have it. I'm sure all of you have your job, hobbies, things you keep for yourself. How about maybe helping her with her thing?" He and the veteran HOTs encouraged "newbies" to start with small stuff, such as helping to carry products to and from the car before or after a party or by simply asking "How was the party?" Even better, they could ask her how she felt overall about her business or what she thought about her team.

At times, Scott strongly urged this crowd of mostly men and husbands to step up in support of their wives as husbands and fathers. He would say things like, "You don't 'babysit' your own kids when your wife is working. You're just being their dad!" Scott would remind them how most women grew up dreaming about marrying someone they looked up to—someone who was their partner and hero. Scott referred to a "knight in shining armor" and he joked, "Look at you . . . I think we all have some work to do in this department!" This, of course, broke the ice and made everyone laugh.

After these conference sessions, Consultants would approach us, often with tears in their eyes, and say things like, "I don't know what you said to my husband in that HOTs class but thank you!" The talks were making a difference in their relationship dynamic around the business. Scott also took great pride in making "big burly dudes" cry, which was something he never had trouble doing. Being married to a man who is secure enough to cry meant being married to someone who was okay with being known as caring and serving too. Scott wanted me to succeed, our Consultants to succeed, and their marriages and families to succeed. He wanted everyone to be *all in,* just like us.

I'll never forget the story about the guy who showed up at one of our annual conference HOTs classes looking, for lack of a better term, "rough." It was obvious he didn't want to be at this "cult conference," as he called it, and he especially didn't want to be in this class of mostly other men. In his case, there also seemed to be something much deeper going on. He stuck it out through the class, then talked briefly to Scott afterward and left a little lighter than when he came in. One year later, in the same HOTs class, a young, energetic, happy guy walked up to Scott with a smile on his face and said, "You don't recognize me, do you?" Scott acknowledged he didn't (I should mention Scott remembers practically *everyone*). It was the "rough" guy from the year before. The guy said something happened to him in that class that changed his life and his marriage, and he had a new life supporting his wife in her successful Thirty-One business. Over the years, stories like this have poured in from husbands and other supporting partners who have gone from "not a fan" to "all in," as they made it a priority to support their wives, their family members, and their friends with their businesses. These stories are some of the greatest emotional blessings on the personal side of this business.

But conference times weren't the only times we were *all in* as a company and as families. We all tried to role model work-life balance, and most importantly, we took the necessary time to be *all in* with our loved ones. At times, the kids grew tired of spending countless hours with us in the office or warehouse. But it was also the place where they had sleepovers on air mattresses while we worked, played GameCube together and learned fun skills like skateboarding and stunt-bike riding. When one of them complained about being there, we reminded them that life wasn't always fair. We can't all do what we want every single day. And we made the conscious choice to support each other as families and as a community.

Scott and I tried to live this out in every area of our lives, not just with Thirty-One. We did our best to show up to all of Alyx's cheer competitions, to help Evan build his skateboards, and be present while on vacation even when our email inboxes were filled to the brim. We made family vacation a priority every year following the annual conference and used Spring Break and winter holidays as a chance to step away from the business and be with our families. We also made adjustments at home by hiring help for household chores and the prep required to host large dinners. Doing so meant we had to get creative with our budget, but it also meant we could show up more present day-to-day with our kids.

A well-rounded, holistic approach to being *all in* is what it ultimately meant for us to be *successful* at Thirty-One. And what a difference this made as we built our business, sold products, planned parties, and gathered our friends.

8

PARTY

Gather Your Friends

WE CHOSE THE DIRECT SALES or party-plan model of business because it supported my *why* to support women and their *whys.* For people who have never been to a direct sales party, assumptions run the gamut. But for us, it was all about gathering our friends. Let me explain what I mean.

A typical Thirty-One party looks something like this: a Consultant asks a friend to host a party by inviting twenty of her friends. We also refer to the host as the "insider" because she (or he) is the *one person* who knows everyone else in the room. The host is also the one who receives special perks without having to join our company as a Consultant. Many women who enjoy this are already gathering for wine nights, game nights, and season-openers or -finales of their favorite TV shows. So, getting together to preview our products is an easy ask for most of them.

In the first 15 years of the company, many of these parties were held in living rooms, on back decks, or around kitchen islands. With busy schedules, not every guest was always available to attend a party in person. But an invitation list of twenty-plus women meant there would likely be at least ten friends who showed up. These parties were full of laughter, fun, and surprises, making for a productive evening for both the host, who had the opportunity to earn our latest products, and our Consultants, who were selling our products.

At most Thirty-One parties, the Consultant shared the latest styles from our most recent seasonal launch, which could be used as gifts, fashion accessories, home decor, or lifestyle organization. That's what we called "solution-selling." Because we are an emotional brand and not just a material brand, we are committed to defining "life solutions" beyond our physical products. For some women in attendance at these parties, our products *are* their solution. The large utility tote is what made packing up for soccer tournaments, sleepovers, or beach days fast and more efficient. For our hosts who gathered friends in their homes, the solution was social time, and free or discounted products earned because her friends were willing to buy products of their own. This meant our hosts got great solutions for their homes without making a dent in their budget. For many women, the solution they discovered at our parties was the opportunity to build their own business, get on their feet financially, and establish a new community of friends.

Another hallmark of our home parties is product demonstration. Most of our products are simple, but our Consultants share stories about how particular products are used to help plan ahead for a busy day of work, activities, or vacation. The Consultants share tips on such things as using our zipper pouches for sunscreen, wet bathing suits, or keeping magazines and personal electronics protected from the water and the sun. This type of solution-oriented selling brought our simple zipper pouch to life.

Consultants continue on to talk about how monogramming zipper pouches distinguish the product "on purpose" as a specific solution. For example, adding monogramming such as "Fun in the Sun" or

"Sunscreen" to the zipper pouches used for water activities or outdoor adventures marked the pouches for specific activities and kept them from being used as a catch-all for extras. And then the Consultant talks about how the styles and prints available in each product give our customers the opportunity to showcase their personalities while taking care of the needs of their families and the necessary activities of their lives. Who wouldn't want to buy our products after that kind of encouraging and empowering conversation?

Being a Thirty-One Consultant allows our women to demonstrate and share unique ideas and the purposeful qualities of our products, but they don't stop there. Many of our Consultants help their hosts and insiders with specific projects, such as pantry makeovers using the half-priced or free items they earned at the party they hosted. The *party* is what made their pantry makeover more affordable, but the *Consultant* is who made the product come to life as a *solution* in the pantry. By helping our customers use our products and find the best solutions for their particular space, we also help their families.

Our personalized organizing products, such as personalized bins for chips, sweets, breakfast, baking, and more, allow a customer to help their kids know where to put things back and keep the pantry organized. Every family needs this kind of help organizing areas of their home. It makes it easy to tell if something is out of place or when groceries are getting low. Better solutions for the home haven't changed over our twenty years of designing, creating, and selling our products party-style, because every home needs organization.

Another area our customers have requested solutions for over the years is organizing the way they travel. It doesn't matter if they are traveling on a plane for Spring Break or driving in the car for work. Having a place for everything—from undergarments and kids' clothes to beauty products and jewelry—makes traveling easier and less stressful. Our products simply help our customers with "life hacks" that enable them to conquer their travel time and ease their busy weeks. From making lunches, creating a drop zone for kids' stuff, getting everyone's gear to the car or loading up for a trip, our products provide easy solutions to these problems. Even better, our products come in fun prints or personalized icons that match their personalities. As our Consultants like to ask at our parties, "Who doesn't want to look good while they're out and about?"

By giving company-wide freedom and encouragement to our Consultants to share their *why* at every party, it elevates the conversation to be about life solutions and purpose, *not* products and pennies. There are so many reasons our Consultants sell our products beyond the products themselves. They boil down to one overarching word: *solutions*. Our Consultants remind their customers of creative ways to make solutions more affordable, such as hosting opportunities, earning insider perks, community connection, and business opportunities for each person who attends one of our parties.

For our Consultants, the party-plan model *is* the solution. It's what helps them consistently meet new friends and customers while continuing to build their businesses. The party, whether in person or through social media, will always include more *sharing* of product solutions rather than *selling* them. We celebrate, encourage, and reward our customers and hosts by doing fun things like asking attendees to share how they know the host and one thing they love about her. Having ten friends celebrate someone publicly is an amazing way to make a person feel good about herself. We also challenge Consultants to share the reason our company exists—to encourage and empower women—as well as share their own personal *why* for being on our team. When customers hear more of the story and heartbeat behind Thirty-One, as well as the impact that party orders had on the host and Consultant, they realize that greater purpose of our Thirty-One family *of encouraging and empowering women.* Our customers have the opportunity to support a real person, along with that person's family and their dreams. This is not a marketing tactic. It is a real-life application of our mission and values.

Eventually, we updated our company mission to reflect the words we share at our parties: *to celebrate, encourage, and reward.* We still have this mission today. Here's how we inspire our community to live out that mission:

Celebrate your accomplishments and who you are as a person.
Encourage your progress with inspirational words and purposeful goals.
Reward your efforts with quality time and amazing incentives.

We found ways to celebrate, encourage, and reward our Consultants as well as help them model this mission with their own customers, insiders, and teams. This is the foundation of everything we did in the beginning, and everything we still do today.

Many of our Consultants have built long-term relationships with customers who come back again and again, and some of our "insiders" host a party with each new catalog release. These relationships are part of what make Thirty-One *more than a bag.* These intrinsic assets and gifts grew their passion for being a Thirty-One Consultant. Our Consultants are proud of the businesses they build as well as the extra income they bring in to help with the family expenses and extras. This in turn builds confidence in our Consultants and make them more eager to share the opportunity with other women looking to add similar benefits to their life.

Our Consultants often join Thirty-One wanting more products or hoping to earn enough money for short-term expenses, like a new couch, tires, braces, or a spring vacation. Once a Consultant is successful with that short-term goal, she realizes she could do more parties and pay off a credit card or save up for a college fund. More than just the money, she connects with others with similar whys or decides she loves being a successful entrepreneur. When a Consultant begins sharing about the Thirty-One business opportunity with other women and helping those women be successful with launching their own businesses, it is not only personally rewarding but also financially rewarding.

Our Consultants came to us with a lot of passion, and in return, we gave them the tools, training, and support they need to reach their goals. Many started as a customer, became a party host, joined our team as a Consultant with a commission plan and incentives, then moved on to be a Leader with a career, free incentive trips, and greater commission opportunities with rising rewards. This was a fast track for so many of them.

It's a good thing they were so passionate because, to be honest, during our first five years, we didn't have the most innovative or best quality products. We didn't have the greatest website or back-office support for our sales teams. The kinds of products we sold were helpful and our systems were important, but those things were not what made Thirty-One a great direct sales company. It was our Consultants and their combination of connections and relationships, and their consistently showing up to serve others that have been our "magic sauce" since the beginning. This relational connection is what has supported every single part of our party-plan business model. Sure, there were other companies we were tracking with at the time, but we knew it was best to distinguish ourselves. The best companies build their business by promoting relationships, regardless of having the best products, systems, and incentives.

The good thing about our industry is that most of us operate with open hands. For that reason, Julie and I were able to attend meetings with other company executives with the Direct Selling Association. We met friends and peers in our Party Plan Council meetings, which were priceless. Sharing ideas with Joan, Nancy, Gretchen, or Asma—women from various direct sales companies—was always inspiring and affirming. And the opportunities to visit the Home Office of Pampered Chef or to have dinner with experts and executives in our industry were helpful as we developed our own vision for growth. We tracked closely with a candle company called Scentsy that launched less than a year after we did. We learned so much from Scentsy founders Orville and Heidi, who are some of our biggest champions. To have such clear insight from other direct sales companies really helped us share our vision and strategy as we planned for more growth.

We also followed the launch of BeautyCounter, Stella & Dot, Origami Owl, Rodan and Fields, and the long-time successes of Pampered Chef and Mary Kay. People used to say I was "the Mary Kay of today"—one of the highest compliments anyone could ever give in the direct sales industry. Mary Kay Ash was a giant in our industry and a role model for every business owner and woman around the world. But we didn't just want to be another great company like Mary Kay, or any other direct selling company. We wanted to make our mark on our own. And we sure did.

Scott used to tell people that we didn't sell products, "we sold hope in a thermal tote." Our bags were game-changers, dream-catchers, peace-keepers, and difference-makers, and they provided a fresh-start solution to frustrating problems for so many. We put a lot of thought and energy into the creation, design, and production of our bags. There was also a lot of passion, purpose, and a heck of a lot of partnerships. When we considered the factories in China helping us create our product, Scott would say, "The countless hands that touch one little bag along its journey is nothing compared to the countless lives it changes." Each bag we created was on a mission to change lives. The life we loved and the life we lived was "in the bag," and it eventually grew to be "more than a bag," one small party at a time.

9

IMAGINE

Define Your Success

SCOTT IS QUICK TO SAY our *purpose* is what drove our success. "Our business wasn't just *our* business—it was *their* business," he says. The women who make up our family of Consultants are what drove the reason we were in business. We existed to empower them, and we wanted them to have fun along the way.

One of our goals for Thirty-One Consultants has been for them to make more money than they spend. That meant our Consultants didn't need closets full of inventory. If they already had a lot of great items to demonstrate at their parties, they were encouraged to sell them, use them for booking more parties, give them away in their "hostess of the month" clubs, or use those products and solutions in whatever ways helped them grow their business and their paycheck. We reminded them of this often. We also referred to this idea as "green activity" and even spent time and energy on focused training to help Consultants with ideas and activities that made money, hence the "green" activities. We also talked to them about how they spent their time online. Were they using all that time online building their businesses or were they using it to scroll on social media for fun, escape, or to engage in politics?

We talked about how "green activity" meant building relationships with their customer groups, promoting great solutions and new products, or talking about the benefits of hosting or joining Thirty-One. Focusing on making more than they were spending wasn't so we could sell a lavish lifestyle or promote the purchase of new cars or homes. This was simply our philosophy. It was our way of encouraging and empowering these women with their own personal return on investment (ROI). If they were going to invest their time, money, and energy into buying a Thirty-One starter kit and starting a business, then we wanted them to earn enough to pay for that kit and pay for the time they spent investing in parties. Of course, some of our Consultants have grown their businesses to lucrative levels of success, but that's not the majority. Many of our Consultants simply love to earn free or discounted products or a little extra money.

Another goal we had was to help our Consultants build the businesses they wanted with the flexibility to do it the way they wanted. I regularly say, "Your pay will match your effort," which is true most of the time. If they invested in running their business with our sales systems of booking parties, coaching insiders, and sharing the Thirty-One opportunity, they could build successful businesses. Yes, there were some Consultants who built their business using mostly online tools, but the age-old "sales funnel" concept was still required in any kind of sales business, including ours. No matter how we built our businesses, we had to have enough new customers coming into the top of the funnel. Parties were always our most valuable and efficient way to meet new customers and fill the sales funnel to help Consultants continue to grow their businesses.

The team has also heard me say a thousand times, "Our product doesn't sell itself." Relationships are the most vital way for our Consultants to build trust and demonstrate our products. Our compensation plan didn't offer a huge base pay, but it allowed us to offer incentives so our Consultants could earn new products for free to show to their customers and earn enough to feel proud about their ROI. If a Consultant made one hundred and fifty dollars for a three- to four-hour party, that was a pretty good ROI. Many of our incentives were set at a level where Consultants could easily make two hundred and fifty dollars, *plus* free products. At that level, our Consultants definitely felt celebrated, encouraged, and rewarded.

Yet another goal we had in helping to shape our success was our monthly sales meetings and our quarterly leadership conferences. Any time we gathered leaders together, we took time to celebrate them and their accomplishments. We encouraged them to dream bigger than ever before in fun and creative ways, and we rewarded them with free products and hope for growth—in relationships, income, and confidence. No one left those gatherings without the courage to take the next step forward in their business, whatever that step might be. We would say, "Imagine what's possible when hundreds and thousands of women are taking the next step toward their goals and dreams!"

I can tell you firsthand, Thirty-One wasn't just a magical moment, it has been a movement. But that movement requires being clear on what it means to be successful. We all had ideas and experiences of what success looked like and meant to each one of us. The Founding Team and growing Executive Team talked about how to keep the Thirty-One momentum alive. We recognized that Thirty-One was *one* thing for someone to do, not the *only* thing. Success meant recognizing that Thirty-One was part of the sum and not the whole.

To remind ourselves of this version of success, we constantly encouraged our community with "leadership lessons." First, we encouraged our Consultants to surround themselves with the sisterhood community of Thirty-One. Next, we asked them to take a few moments to write down where they wanted to stay focused and committed. We asked them, "What are you doing to make time for beyond Thirty-One?" For me, it was my faith and family. We directed them to create a plan by asking, "How are you prioritizing your time, energy, and activities in addition to Thirty-One?" Let's take Scott for example: his priorities were faith and family too, but his plan was to move people—with music, his inspirational talks, and his pastoral care. This is how we helped our Consultants develop a practical plan for their own success.

Most people think happiness is the definition of success. But I believe success is moving one step forward. We are successful as individuals in big and small ways every time we learn something new, set a new goal, work to achieve it, and get curious about something beyond what we know to be true. So many of our Consultants were classroom teachers. But the fact is, we were ALL students. Maybe some of our women didn't do well in school (like me), and that defined their lives for so long. But as adults, we get to define what success looks like for each one of us. We could play to our strengths, rather than be defined by our failures and weaknesses. No matter how you slice it, playing to your strengths always brings some form of success. We get to measure ourselves to the purpose God put inside of each one of us, which means we can let go of other people's standards and narrow definitions of success to make room for our own.

In addition to having the habit of moving one step forward, I have found success in surrounding myself with amazing people who love to be successful. I have often shared, "Surround yourself with people who help you see what success looks like for you." I believe mentors are important, but I am not one who looks up to big celebrities, public figures, or business executives. I love real-life people who are doing life with me, people who are vulnerable about their struggles yet continue to chase their dreams.

God has blessed me with so many people in my life. My friend Pam, for example, helped me grow as a young woman in my 20s, from having kids to becoming an entrepreneur. My friend Andrea was another person God sent my way at the peak of my career. She taught me to always be a learner, to be myself as I was leading, and that it's okay to be vulnerable. My mom taught me the value of hard work as well as many lessons about transition. And "Ger," my mother-in-law, has taught me to love better, not judge, and be patient and forgiving.

I have shared many times with our leaders at Thirty-One about how we can be intentional about who we surround ourselves with in life. Just like the images we carefully and thoughtfully place on our personal vision boards; we can choose who we spend time with and how we want to show up as a result of the encouragement and inspiration from our people. This is what I refer to as my "life board." But I haven't always shown up with an open mind to learn; it's something I've developed as I've gotten older. We all have many teachers in our lives, and those teachers are not always at the front of a classroom. They are everyday people like you and me. Then and now, I wanted to be a lifelong student and keep on learning and growing. I still pray that God never stops sending me teachers, friends, and mentors to help me live out my purpose.

That's a bit about my personal definition of success, but if we were to also look at our success as a company by the world's standards, then most people would see that we've done quite well. We have always tried to make our decisions in such a way that they ultimately help others keep taking positive steps forward. And in return, our Consultants, hosts, customers, and employees have all helped us break incredible records. For example:

> We eventually grew to reach almost $800 million annually, projected to hit one billion dollars in sales in a single year by our industry followers, a target we have yet to reach. (Very few direct sales companies go past *$50 million* or even break *$100 million* in a year.)
>
> At one point, we had over 100,000 Consultants, coming from every state and several provinces in Canada, but predominantly located on the East Coast.
>
> We grew to over one million social media followers on Facebook and Instagram. We had tons of media attention and sold more products than I could have ever dreamed.

I never imagined that we would reach the eventual level of success we did because I never defined success based on a number of Consultants, sales, or profitability.

Defining our success in every new season of our business meant we often had to figure out a better plan to make sure we were taking the right next steps forward. By nature, I'm a planner. I actually enjoy it! Some of you can identify with me, while others may think I'm weird. I enjoy every single part of it: planning time to plan, planning the people to plan with, the planning itself, then executing the plan. I also love having a partner who can keep up with all the planning I like to do, and for me, that partner has been Julie Sutton. Julie has been engaged in everything from the very beginning, including catalog development and execution, strategic planning offsites to staff meetings, and so much more. She was my original business partner and is still a vital part of the success of Thirty-One. I could have never executed all those plans without her.

We learned fast that no matter what size our business was, if we wanted to be successful, we had to have goals and a plan. I'll admit that in the beginning, it was more about taking risks as an entrepreneur than having a big multi-year strategy as a CEO. And it was a big risk in those days to try selling giftables, purses, totes, and thermals in a direct selling home party-plan model. Sure, we had mini-goals in those early days, like having a catalog, showing up at our first vendor event, and holding a few home parties. We even had a short-term business plan and decent products, but I wouldn't say we had a well-thought-out strategy until we began finding success.

A couple of years into the business, as we were growing superfast, we took a long weekend to plan. We had just moved the business out of my basement, employed several friends (remember the Founding Mothers?), and bought a few monogram machines. But I knew we had to be more efficient. We needed to find creative ways to get more production out of our machines, more orders out the door, and more customer support calls answered. We didn't really have the time or the money to take a long weekend for strategic planning, but it seemed like the right kind of splurge. So, Julie, Cathy, Kim, and I packed up our families and went to Pigeon Forge, Tennessee. We rented a house at the edge of town in nearby Townsend, Tennessee, to save money. The dads took care of the kids while the moms worked on plans to be more efficient and support the crazy business growth we were seeing.

Julie was the one helping me with our sales forecast. She and I knew we were growing month over month, and it wasn't slowing down. We didn't want to invest in more machines or people, but we knew we needed to create short-term *and* longer-term plans to support the growth. Cathy helped us with the operational strategic plan to get more units out the door, including more shipments sent out during our peak at the end of every month. Kim was there to help us with feedback from the sales field and help prevent missing orders and wrong monograms that our Consultants were calling about. She was running our Consultant support team, which meant the ability to gracefully field calls and respond to the missteps and hiccups we were experiencing with our growing pains.

We also put together a sales field group of ten Consultants at the time and called them our Presidential Advisory Council. During the transition to our second warehouse space in Hixson, we invited the council to see our new space before we moved into it. We were so excited to do a ribbon-cutting ceremony that we didn't pay much attention to the lack of cleanliness. During our building tour, there was a dead rat on the warehouse floor that Scott and Julie hid by standing in front of it, just as the group rounded the corner to the warehouse. We were grossed out then, but we often laugh about it now.

Here's how Julie remembers those early planning days:

> With strategic planning at the top of our mind for how we would continue to manage the growing business and make it function as smoothly as possible, we set aside several days to get away for a planning retreat at the base of the Smoky Mountains. Hunkered down in a remote cabin next to the Little River with our families, it was our mission to plan for our ever-growing business without interruptions.
>
> Upon arrival, we were met by a utility worker who was supposedly there to fix something at the house. You can imagine our jitters as we walked into a dark cabin in the woods, hoping the utility guy was telling the truth and was not some burglar. But it turned out to be a quaint spot for our retreat. We spent the first evening talking, laughing, playing cards, and overall, just decompressing from the busyness of everything. The next morning, we woke up to see the river for the first time. It was a beautiful but chilly February morning, so we spent most of our day inside the cabin figuring our way through our first strategic planning session.
>
> One of the challenges we faced with a larger facility was that we needed some processes put in place. We had more of everything: more machines, more products, more shipping boxes, more people.

And we had to figure out a better flow. This is where we established our "zones" process flow that we used for the next several years in the business. We outlined how the process flow should work from the time an order was received on our website to the time it was packed up and shipped out the door.

- **ZONE 1** was where the orders were printed.
- **ZONE 2** was where the products that needed to be personalized were picked up from the warehouse floor for processing.
- **ZONE 3** was where the embroidery was added to the products.
- **ZONE 4** was where the non-personalized products were added to the order.
- And so on with **ZONES 5-8**.
- **ZONE 9**, the last zone, was the shipping label station where the boxes were taped closed and stacked on a pallet.

Zones were necessary so we could avoid incorrect orders going out the door as much as possible. All of our orders had to go out to the warehouse, then back into the office area for personalization, then back to the warehouse for processing. And zones were our way of doing this efficiently with quality checks along the way.

We were proud of the outcome of our planning meeting that year, as it was going to help set us up for additional business growth that we had no idea we were ever going to experience.

As always with Thirty-One, it was important for us to stop working and enjoy some downtime with our families as we wrapped up our planning that weekend. The kids skipped stones in the river and jumped from boulder to boulder. It was chilly outside, but the family time together was unforgettable. We drove to Pigeon Forge for every kind of activity you could imagine and opted for Go-Karts since all the kids were old enough to ride along with one of the adults. We laughed so hard when we realized that the cold weather left us with frozen snot-faced kids after a few turns around the outdoor track. We had so much fun!

Eventually, once we built a business infrastructure and Home Office team to support a more than seven-hundred million-dollar business, it was hard to figure out how to keep defining our success and making the best plan for the next step required to keep us moving forward. At some point, we had to right-size the business as sales began to slow down into a more natural stride, and we began to experience more attrition with our sellers—both of which are normal and natural in a sales cycle like ours. More on this later. What I want you to know is that defining our success was both fun and challenging, but it often took more energy than we had. It was so crucial for us to include other people in the process of defining our success and imagining the future of Thirty-One. We constantly had to figure out what it took to keep growing so we could maintain our success.

10

GROW

Figure Out What It Takes

OUR GROWTH, as well as our growing pains, continued beyond our first strategic planning event in Townsend as we regularly had to move our products and monogramming machines to offices more suitable for our latest expansion. Unfortunately, the new spaces were not always sufficient for our growth over the following month.

To alleviate some of the tension, we ordered more monogramming machines, and Cathy trained new monogrammers weekly. Thanks to Atrium, we had the opportunity to begin creating our own Thirty-One branded products. Plus, we officially had a best-selling product: the thermal tote. Atrium made this classic item in exclusive prints unique to our product line. And we figured out small tricks of the trade to make our products even more desirable, such as adding a pocket to the front of the thermal tote to make it easier to monogram.

Through all those early days of constant change and growth, we saw God's hand working out details along the way. For our first big shipment of exclusive Thirty-One products, Atrium called to say the shipment was on its way and would require 10,000 square feet to store it. We did not have that kind of space available at our old warehouse in Tennessee. Randomly, we received a call that same day from our landlord's office saying our next-door business neighbor, with whom we shared a wall, had moved. We were offered an additional 10,000 square feet of space, and they were willing to give us a deal on it and knock a hole in the wall. I'll never forget the look on our Atrium partner's face when he said, "Your God is looking out for you!" We didn't always have a plan, but we kept moving forward, leaning into our faith and trusting that God did have one.

As we began to order more and more products from Atrium, I wanted to see the factories producing our goods. I needed to make sure they had enough capacity to support our demand for the present and future. So, in 2008, I took my first trip to China, and it changed everything for me. I met the owner of the main sewing factory where our products were made. The entire team was so welcoming and kind. On a day I will never forget, the owner took me on a tour, and in one of the production rooms, I saw mounds of Thirty-One products for our next season. I was overwhelmed as I stood there trying to take it all in. Even as I flew home, I could not get this vision out of my mind. I realized our company was growing bigger than we could continue to support in Chattanooga. We needed a new plan.

Scott and I had recently built a new home but were still adding finishing touches. When I got home, Scott had me close my eyes for him to make a big reveal: a built-in closet set from Ikea. I opened my eyes, sat down, and cried. Through tears, I told Scott that we couldn't stay in the house. We needed to move for the business. It was too big for Soddy Daisy, Tennessee. Now *he* was overwhelmed. We discussed if the possibility made sense.

I decided to post our open jobs, which were growing by the week, in Atlanta, Georgia, and Columbus, Ohio. Columbus was where our new product-sourcing partners at Atrium were located. Julie and I had been there a few times on product development trips. Not only was our product partner in Columbus, but there was also a long history of direct sales industry talent. Columbus was home to the iconic direct sales company, Longaberger handcrafted baskets, so people were quite familiar with our industry.

It was September, and our kids had just started back to school. Scott and I knew if we were serious about the expansion of our Home Office into Columbus, we needed to get our feet on the ground and carry our company culture into the new offices. Time was of the essence, so Scott and I took a weekend trip to visit Columbus. After that, our conversations quickly escalated, and within three weeks we made our decision. We would move the business to Ohio, sell our newly finished home, and enroll our kids in a new school. We pulled our team together to share the news and invited them to join us in Columbus, but made certain they knew it was not mandatory. We needed to take it one step at a time, and in that moment, the best next step was opening a Home Office and warehouse space in a city primed for the direct sales industry.

A few weeks later, fully uprooted to Ohio, we took a walk on a nearby nature trail in New Albany, fifteen miles from Columbus. Scott and I were tearful watching our kids and realizing we were starting a completely new life, away from our family and Southern roots, all for the sake of our dream for Thirty-One. This was an important time in which I had a short-term plan with long-range goals. I had to act quickly without looking back for a single second. It proved to be the right move in many ways.

Here's Cathy's take on the move:

> The move to Ohio was very emotional. It meant pulling our kids away from family and friends in Tennessee at such crucial ages. Savannah was a junior in high school, and Dakota was going into seventh grade. My husband had a good job as an electrical contractor, and in the past,

we had moved for his job. This was the first time we would be moving for my job.

We visited Ohio in March 2009 over Spring Break. Then, after much thought, prayer, and family discussion, we moved to Ohio that July. It was difficult, but we felt like it was good for our family and for the larger purpose of serving others through Thirty-One. The Monroes and Suttons were there before us, and since our families are really close, we were all in it together. We had each other for support through the transition.

Our family moved to Granville, Ohio, which is a "Mayberry"-type town northeast of the new Home Office in the Johnstown/Columbus area. We could walk down Main Street to restaurants, pick up frozen custard for dessert, visit the drugstore for last-minute school supplies, and stop by the bank and post office on the way home. My true welcome to Ohio came following an ACL injury from jumping on a trampoline with the kids two weeks after we arrived. So it was a slow start to a fast season of life.

Our house became one of the hangouts for other Tennessee families who also moved north. We hosted a Halloween event in which all the families came over for trick-or-treating together, followed by pizza and dessert. We also hosted an annual Christmas event featuring a walk through downtown Granville to see the lighted trees, a parade with Santa, ice sculptures, cookie decorating, kettle-corn vendors, and so much more. And we loved the Granville Fourth of July celebration highlighted by a parade and carnival that lasted four days.

We built traditions in Ohio with our Tennessee friends, and Consultants would come to stay with us during these fun times.

We kept our Chattanooga, Tennessee, facility for two more years while we were building a new office and warehouse facility in Ohio. In 2009, we built our first company owned Thirty-One building in Johnstown, Ohio. But before construction was even completed, we had already outgrown it and had to rent additional space next door. That was how fast we were growing. We made the decision to close our distribution center in Tennessee and move it all to Ohio. We asked the rest of our Tennessee employees if they would be willing to move north, knowing this was the best way to have a seamless transition between locations and operations. Nearly 20 families voluntarily decided to join us in Ohio, which helped us maintain a strong sense of Thirty-One culture in the new space. Of course, it also helped us keep orders going out the door with a core team who knew how we did things and worked fast.

Here's how Julie remembers that time:

> As would be expected with the growth we experienced, we wanted to have our own building. So in 2009, we purchased thirty-one acres (of course) across the street from the Atrium building, and broke ground as soon as it thawed enough for construction to begin. Our new office address was 231 with a zip code of 43031. How could that not feel like God was winking at all of us? Those months of watching the Thirty-One building go up and seeing the results were so exciting. We finally had our own space with room for all the celebrations we had started during our Tennessee days.

Business continued to grow, and soon we were busting at the seams again in Johnstown. That's when we moved our offices and operations into the former Victoria's Secret Catalog building in Columbus in the fall of 2010. The space was way too big, but we were tired of moving every year or two, and we knew it could hold everything. The parent company, L Brands, had plans to tear it down, but we made an offer to pay all the taxes and take care of all maintenance in exchange for using the space. They agreed. It was the perfect home for us because we could have our entire team, including our offices and operations, all in one place.

I took another trip to China to ensure the quality and color of our bags and to continue building relationships with the factory owners.

By this time, more than ninety percent of our products were being sourced through Atrium and their amazing team, including Andy, David, and Douglas. We were all up for the challenge of growing one hundred to three hundred percent year over year. Atrium helped us focus on better quality, product innovation, and expanding the number of factories to ensure we had plenty of capacity.

Sales forecasting became super important, which meant we had to hire the right people to help with inventory planning. Funding the growth was a challenge. Fast growth required all our cash to go back into the business to pay for bigger quantities of inventory, larger warehouses, and more talent.

As we were growing, evolving, and hiring more team members, I started counting on others to handle important parts of the business. My role had naturally evolved from doing everything with a small team to managing a medium-size company, to leading a large-scale profitable business. By 2009, we had 12,000 Consultants and, by 2010, we were up to 25,000 women selling our bags and building their own businesses. Without time to stop and do any kind of leadership training, I soaked up leadership books like a sponge as I figured out how to grow and keep up as a leader. All this business growth and the personal growth I wanted to do required a lot of time and energy. We had meetings to build annual plans, seasonal plans, monthly plans, and weekly reactions to sales.

Thankfully, Julie and I were leading the planning together. Here's what she had to say about it:

> Cindy's move to Ohio didn't immediately impact the rest of the Chattanooga employees. But we knew there would come a time when we would have to make the decision to move to Ohio or leave Thirty-One. Between 2009 and 2010, an offer was extended to anyone wanting to make the move, and around twenty team members joined us in Ohio.

> I was the first to agree to move my family, and it was not an easy decision. Thankfully, my kids were only three and six at the time; others had older kids and teenagers to consider. Never before had we lived away from our parents or extended family, but we truly believed this was the right choice. Jason lost his dad in 2008, and that life-altering experience made it easier for us to decide, as did the fact we had poured so much into Thirty-One for more than five years at that point. We determined that Jason would leave his job as a graphic designer and be the stay-at-home parent. Jordan finished kindergarten in Chattanooga before we moved to New Albany, Ohio, in June 2009.
>
> Our families were supportive but hesitant to understand why we felt the move to Columbus was necessary. Having seen us work so hard over years helped them see that we truly believed in what we were doing. The fact that co-workers who were also some of our closest friends were willing to move eased the pain of leaving home. We found a church we attended with some of our Tennessee families, and we bonded over a Sunday lunch group we called "Praise the Lord and pass the biscuits." We rotated homes and had fun gathering as families who were experiencing similar challenges. As a result, our kids grew even closer.

I was so grateful for Julie and her natural ability to stay one step ahead of everyone. She was the reason we were always ready for new catalogs, monthly specials, and communication plans. But it felt like the more people who got involved in the growth and strategy of the business, the more mistakes we made. We did our best to collaborate and redefine roles, but we were moving so fast it became a bit chaotic at times.

That's where Cathy stepped in to care for our employee team. Her role had already morphed into Human Resources before we moved to Ohio. We weren't sure she and her family were going to make the move, but we were so thankful when they did. In Tennessee, Cathy was the kind of HR leader who saw when our employees were wearing down in the heat of the warehouse or freezing in the cold. She would bring ice pops and extra water on hot days, and hot chocolate and heaters on cold ones. She had the idea to shuttle employees to the warehouse when there was a flood in our parking lot. And at the end of most workdays, you could find her at the clock-out computer thanking our employees for a job well done and telling them just how much we appreciate them. This was Cathy. And she was a vital part of what it took to successfully transition our team from Tennessee to Ohio.

PART TWO

Chasing the Ball Downhill

Success doesn't come from what you choose to do occasionally. It comes from what you choose to do consistently.

—MARIE FORLEO

11

MOMENTUM

Here We Go

OUR REMARKABLE GROWTH was getting attention from the press as well as the Columbus business community. We were being mentioned and profiled in leadership and business magazines and, thanks to our fast growth, making all "the lists," including *Ernst & Young, Forbes,* the *Columbus Fast 50,* and many other points of recognition. We have talked about growth, but without details, it's hard to imagine. So here is a snapshot of the growth in our Thirty-One Consultant timeline during our first ten years:

2003: 1
2004: 20
2005: 50
2006: 250
2007: 1500
2008: 4,000
2009: 12,000
2010: 25,000
2011: 60,000
2012: 90,000
2013: 113,000
2014: 106,000

This incredible growth resulted in massive hiring. We hired a VP of Finance and Operations and a VP of Sales and Customer Service Associates, who worked out of our new location. Our Operations Team was growing as well. Every week, we were hiring and training new monogrammers and employees for shipping, quality control, information technology, and just about every other department. We kept all our essential operations in-house when other companies our size were outsourcing departments and service areas such as call center, marketing, sales, finance/accounting, technology, operations, people development, and organizational culture.

After we settled in Columbus, I knew it was important to schedule an offsite planning meeting with our newer Executive Team. Several team members were given opportunities to travel to China. Whenever they did, they came home with more vision and passion for our work to encourage and empower women and their families around the globe. One year, Scott helped me plan a leadership team trip that included tours of Koehler and Miller Brewing Company and Harley Davidson, all great companies with longstanding family brands and amazing organizational cultures. Our purpose on this trip was to focus on our brand and get clear on what set us apart.

That's when we settled on our twelve values. These were the words and behaviors that reflect our faith, integrity, and the culture of being others-focused—the foundation of our entire mission. I had been around the block enough to know that companies try to create new values to build a culture. We used our existing culture to cement our values. The culture at Thirty-One has always been our greatest asset, and I believe it will continue to set us apart and lead us forward. Chapter 30 has a list of our values and much more about them.

At one point, our rapid growth meant we had to put a pause on recruiting so we could plan for better processes and products before adding more Consultants to our team. The sales growth was exciting, but it felt like we were chasing a ball downhill. Believe me when I say it wasn't always easy chasing the ball downhill. The Call Center had long wait times, and with all the new people in operations, there were products missing from orders, including bags and hostess items. We were working with new factories, and they were rushing to ship products to us, resulting in quality and service issues. Because of the growth and ever-increasing commission checks for our Consultants, they showed us a lot of grace with these challenges.

In the middle of what often felt like mayhem, we had an amazing customer special: If a customer spent thirty-one dollars on an order, they got a zipper pouch for one dollar. We quickly sold out of the zipper pouches and had *thousands* of backorders that took a long time to fulfill. We refer to that season as "Zippergate." More on this later, but the point I'm trying to make is that massive growth, which resulted in the feeling of constantly chasing a ball downhill, was sometimes painful. I'd be lying if I didn't say there were times when we lost sleep over things like zipper pouches and backorders. But we made our way through, and when we did, we took time to celebrate with high fives and big sighs.

While staying on top of staffing and hiccups with our sales and new products, we developed tools to help our Consultants. These tools constantly evolve to meet whatever challenges and opportunities we face. For years, we had the standard set of training videos, recruitment brochures, seasonal catalogs, and monthly special fliers. Those tools proved invaluable during our rapid growth, and we have constantly developed and tweaked them.

There was, however, an "elephant in the room" when it came to marketing and communication tools we weren't ready to address. It seemed everyone in direct sales outside of Thirty-One was talking about a particular new sales method that we were deliberately cautious and skeptical about it. It was the big new monster of *social media.* Facebook had been around for a while, and Instagram and Twitter were gaining steam as sales platforms. Although we all had these basic social accounts as individuals and as a company, we hadn't figured out how to leverage social media as a tool for our Thirty-One home parties.

Like the rest of the world, we loved reconnecting with family and friends; seeing pictures of what they had for breakfast, lunch, and dinner on any given day; and gloating over videos of their kid's Little League power swing. But social media scared us when we considered how we could use it as a tool for our company. I'll be the first to admit, social media often left me distracted. Scott used to say that giving people a way to say whatever they wanted, however they wanted to say it for everyone to see was a little like handing a loaded weapon to a toddler. Nothing good was going to come from it in the long run.

From a business perspective, as long as we could control the script and narrative of Thirty-One on paper, we could mostly maintain the gracious culture and professional way our Consultants represented the brand. Giving our Consultants the keys to share our Thirty-One business brand over their personal social media accounts was terrifying. But it was just the unknown that scared us. As things often go, we knew we had to either adapt and move on or get stuck and wonder where everyone else went. So we eventually figured out how to leverage this Wild West of social media as a business tool for our brand.

We did our best to make the transition to selling via social media while still prioritizing the face-to-face business model that built deep friendships and generated successful businesses at our end. We reminded our Consultants and ourselves that Facebook "friends" weren't automatically real friends. We had to work at those relationships. We also reminded each other that the lives we saw being lived online were only a tiny sliver of reality, and there was so much more both good and bad, in the non-public facing parts of our real lives. I wish I could say we have loved every minute of our foray into social media sales.

Our Consultants began connecting with old friends and new acquaintances online. Social media was a great option in parts of the country where it isn't common to simply drop by at a stranger's home. In the South, all you have to do is show up with sweet tea, baked goods, and a new product catalog, and you're friends for life. It's not the same in other parts of the country. Social media also could enable a Consultant who lives in a town with only a single four-way-stop intersection to expand her reach and business. And for our ladies who are shy, the buffer of the computer gave them confidence and comfort.

Eventually, social media had plenty of positive outcomes for our Consultants and their businesses, but many not-so-positive ones as well. Some of our older Consultants felt left behind when we opened the floodgates of social media sales, while the younger generation was more technologically savvy. They understood the game of algorithms, paid boosting of posts, the use of multiple profiles, and any number of ways to make "the system" work in their favor. We supported our Consultants as they dealt with nasty things said on social media, either about them or our products. The old saying "hurt people hurt people" came way before the time of social media, but it still rings loud and true. People say the meanest things online these days. And it can take only one vindictive person or someone who has misunderstood a situation to compromise the reputation of one of our Consultants or our brand. We added a new topic of conversation to every team meeting, sales training, and conference: Social Media

Etiquette. And our advice was simple: Don't be THAT girl. Don't be that girl on social media who spreads negativity and puts other people down only to put yourself ahead. That's not who we are as a company, and that's not the kind of person we want on our team.

For all its challenges and considerations, selling our products on social media eventually became a necessity when COVID-19 hit in 2020. Not only was it our main method for selling, but it also became essential for recruiting brand ambassadors and Consultants. It was the single greatest tool that sustained our business during the pandemic. Many Consultants who had never used social media learned to adapt. It became the lifeline to keep their business going through quarantines, mandates, and surges of the virus. We learned that sometimes a less-than-favorite tool can become your most critical ally.

Staying flexible and trying new things was critical to maintaining the momentum that was building in our business—momentum we couldn't have planned even if we had tried. All we had to do was respond, and the best way was to double-down on what made our company culture so unique as we grew: to celebrate, encourage, and reward every individual, every milestone, and every new season of momentum.

12

CELEBRATE

Have Fun

FROM 2008 TO 2012, as we settled into operations in Ohio and were still growing like crazy, our momentum made us feel we were on top of the world. Yet that season of exponential growth came with challenges. Then these hurdles, in turn, gave way to a very special season at Thirty-One. Through it all, we were committed to creating space for our people to have fun and celebrate. Our approach was part of our philosophy that we wanted our employees leaving each day feeling fulfilled so they could be better people at home. To us, family came first. Scott encouraged our team that, if they got a call from a family member during a meeting, to step out and take the call. He always assured them that we didn't want them to carry stress home from work.

We made time for fun every chance we got. Scott jokes about how we "built our company on Chick-fil-A Chick-n-Minis and sweet tea" because he always showed up at New Employee Orientation with a tray of them. There were winter days when an announcement over the warehouse PA system invited everyone outside for a snowman-building contest. We had ping-pong tables for lunch-break tournaments in our operations area, and we hosted chili cookoffs, philanthropic golf tournaments, departmental pumpkin-decorating contests, and so much more.

At times, the Thirty-One team would spontaneously spring a fun idea on our employees. One afternoon Scott was giving a tour of the facility when he noticed that, oddly, none of the monogramming machines were running. He found the monogramming team, including supervisors, having a contest from the warehouse mezzanine to see whose paper airplane made the best landing on the factory floor below. With pride and a mischievous smile, Scott turned to our guests and said, "You know, nothing is so important that we can't take a few minutes to have a little fun."

Pranks in the offices were a big thing too. There are dozens of stories about the McDonald's cheeseburger that made the rounds for years (I kid you not, *years*) hidden in desk drawers in the marketing offices. Employees were known to return from vacation to find their office cube and desk accessories covered in plastic wrap. One time, Scott's office was filled front to back and top to bottom with our signature pink boxes. And I once bought a bunch of Nerf guns for impromptu battles with the marketing and sales teams. CEOs can be fun sometimes too. *Right?*

We took time every month to celebrate. My sweet assistant, Jane, would pop into my office like clockwork to remind me when it was time to observe birthdays and work anniversaries. Everyone, and I mean *everyone*, would congregate in the big break room in the middle of the warehouse first floor. I don't remember missing more than one or two monthly celebrations in all those years. Our Leadership Team would assemble at the front of the gathering to form a high-five line, one of our favorite traditions at Thirty-One. Music played as slides on a big screen showed pictures of the employees being celebrated and members of a selected department read the names. The honorees would walk, strut, run, or dance through their eight hundred co-workers as they made their way to the high-five line.

I loved looking around that big room in those moments, seeing the faces smiling, toes tapping, hands clapping, and hips swaying as they danced to the music and celebrated their fellow employees. After the last person made their way through the high-five line, the house band played, and we had all sorts of fun games and activities: baton twirling, hula hooping, special appearances from The Ohio State University mascot "Brutus the Buckeye," and surprise visits from our Consultants who showed up to express their gratitude. One time the finance team put on their favorite animal mask for a "What Did the Fox Say" Flash Mob. To simply tell you how much we valued taking time to celebrate each other at Thirty-One seems like a massive understatement compared to what it was like to be in the room during those parties. Not only did we celebrate the people, but we also celebrated the impact we were having collectively on the families of everyone who loved working at Thirty-One.

The celebration didn't end with the party. We handed out cupcakes to everyone on their way back to their cubicle, office, shipping station, or sewing machine. Most months we had cupcake flavors that still make my mouth water today, such as Cookies & Cream, Peanut Butter & Jelly, and my favorite Strawberry. The individuals being celebrated got to visit the "Celebration Closet" and pick out a free Thirty-One product. Believe it or not, even the men loved this. They would often pick out something for their spouse, kids, or mother.

I know all of you finance people are reading this part and doing the math. Yep, you guessed it: We had eight hundred-plus employees being paid to party for thirty minutes on the clock, plus cupcakes, party supplies, music, and free products. It may have seemed like an unnecessary expense in the moment, but it was priceless for making our people feel celebrated and maintaining a fun organizational culture.

Another favorite tradition was our Thanksgiving celebration. This started as a small potluck and grew to an eight-hundred employee celebration. Many of our managers proudly wore their Thirty-One aprons and served our employees a traditional Thanksgiving meal of turkey, dressing, gravy, green beans, mashed potatoes, pie, and tea (both sweetened and unsweetened). I'm not typically a big fan of a buffet-style meal, but this one was so good. And like any other Thirty-One celebration, there was always good music playing in the background. Once everyone went through the buffet line and was seated, Scott would say the blessing, not just for the food or the business. Scott prayed for God to bless our employees, their families, and the work we were all doing to have a greater impact on empowering our Consultants and their families.

This was one of many, many times throughout the year that I was given the chance to say thank you. I'm not sure if it was because I had done almost every job in the company or if it was because I knew so many of our employees, but these were emotional moments for me, and I'm not one easily moved to tears. Those moments were emotional because I hoped that each person knew I genuinely was thankful that they showed up every day to live out the mission of Thirty-One with me. It was our opportunity to give back to our community and serve other people together. That's what brought tears to my eyes.

I'm sure on occasion the Thanksgiving meal came with a discussion of company updates or "housekeeping" items, but rarely did anyone miss this time or even get up to go to the bathroom during the meal because they didn't want to miss the best part of our tradition: gift-giveaways! We gave away gas cards, grocery cards, iPads, gaming stations, and a couple of what I call (all in one breath) big-daddy-large-screen TVs. We took our managers' names out of the drawings because they expressed that they wanted their team members to have more of a chance to win. When names were called, especially for the big-ticket items, we all celebrated. Responses were priceless: some people laughed in disbelief that they won, some cried, and others danced their way up to receive their gift with their hands waving in the air. At the end of our Thanksgiving celebration, everyone was given the gift of a Thirty-One product, which served as a reminder that we all made it through another year of business together. We left that lunch filled not only with food, but also with joy, pride. and so much gratitude.

There were other celebrations that Cathy remembers so well:

"UNDER THE BIG TOP"—In the spring of 2010 after moving into our new building in Johnstown, Ohio, we decided to have an appreciation event for our employees and their families. It was circus-themed with big white tents decorated with balloons, a delicious catered meal, and lots of fun games for the kids. We made special T-shirts that most of us admit having kept for years. It was a fun-filled day of laughter, good food, connection, and new friends.

CHILI COOK-OFF—There's nothing like fall in the Midwest as the weather cools down and football ramps up. We took this time as an opportunity to have a company-wide chili cook-off before we were swamped with holiday sales. Everyone who wished to participate signed up to make their favorite chili and provided recipes on index cards for those who wanted to duplicate their efforts and provide more food. On the day of the cook-off, tables were lined up along the walls with tons of crock pots full of a variety of chilies. We all met in the common area to try a few before votes were cast and winners were announced. The best part was bragging rights for having everyone's favorite recipe.

BREAKFAST PANCAKES—There's no better way to say thank you to the home team than with a hearty breakfast. The motto for our annual breakfasts was: "We flip 'em! You catch 'em." Employees stood in line while the cook flipped pancakes to whomever was up next. Thankfully, most people were intent on catching pancakes on their plate (versus letting them drop to the floor) before adding syrup and toppings at the breakfast bar. Then everyone took time to sit, eat, and connect. And it was just as much fun as it sounds!

Of course, the Home Office wasn't the only area of the business where we loved bringing the fun. Outside of our employee celebrations, our annual National Conference was the most fun and celebratory event of the year for our Consultants. We called it our Thirty-One Super Bowl. The celebration started in the parking lot, where we had a welcoming team even before our Consultants made it to the registration tables. Once the ladies were checked in, they assembled their name tags and lanyards with all of their ribbons. Ribbons were, and still are, a big deal because they were a visible sign of what each Consultant accomplished with her sales goals. Then we spent the next three days together celebrating our successes and having all kinds of good-natured fun.

Besides the National Conference, many of our team would also travel to towns across the country to meet with our Consultants and sales leaders to celebrate them in person. We rented out theaters across the United States every spring to show a ninety-minute video to reveal new products and prints, introduce our Home Office leaders, and highlight the heart-felt stories of our Consultants. One video premiere included our Communications Director Kate Hannum-Rose (affectionately known by our team as "Communi-Kate") and Mark Carr, one of our sales coaches, driving an RV across the country as they talked about our new Thirty-One products. Although the RV adventure looked real, the actual filming occurred in our warehouse with special effects that made it look like the RV was bouncing down the road and traveling across the country.

Scott and I couldn't make it to every town to celebrate with our Consultants, but each year we picked a location and surprised a group at their local theater. Usually, the theater manager and one of our local leaders would sneak us in the back door of the theater so we could walk in right before the film was about to roll. I would yell "Hey, Ladies...", which they knew that voice and phrase so well, and the crowd would immediately scream and begin clapping. Within minutes, I had texts from other leaders that were so happy one of their team members was in the audience. We would sit in the front of the theater with a few leaders as we watched the film. Scott and I loved listening to the audience "ooh" and "ahh" over new products and laugh at the jokes of the video hosts. Then, after the showing, I would stand to thank the Consultants and meet as many of them as possible. These surprise celebrations were some of my favorites.

Because I believe in our business and love our products, I was *always* ready to celebrate every time I traveled somewhere for a business meeting, even on our family vacations. During one family trip to Hawaii, we decided at the last minute to meet our Hawaiian Thirty-One Consultants and leaders in Honolulu. We called them our *o'hana,* which means "family" in Hawaiian. In 2016, when Alyx was visiting potential colleges, we got to stop and visit with a few of our amazing leaders and Consultants along the way, all of whom offered to be a mom-away-from-Mom for her if she were to choose the local school in their area. (I think the idea of Jen Cornell being a stand-in mom was far more appealing to Alyx than attending Elon, which she didn't pick.) Our Consultants have always been an incredible personal support net for us wherever we go. And of course, there were times when a Consultant spotted me at Disney World or at the airport where I was always up for hugs, photos, meeting each other's kids, and comparing our Thirty-One bags. Spontaneous celebrations like that are the highlights of my days!

Occasionally, a few of the Founding Mothers slipped away with our families for a little fun. After all, we encouraged everyone in our company to enjoy life and focus on the positive as our way of defining what it meant to be fun-loving. In the winter of 2011, Julie, Cathy, Kim, and I took our families on a ski trip getaway. There were sixteen of us in total, and we had such a fun time. We made the best memories on the snow-tubing hill as we rode down together—each of us in a single tube and all holding hands. We did this over and over and over and had a hilariously good time. Our kids still talk about it when we're all together.

Celebrations were what helped us have fun and what kept our feet on the ground during those fast and furious days. But we didn't have fun just to have fun. We had fun because we believed it was essential to our overall mission of encouraging and empowering women.

13

ENCOURAGE

Better Together

THE "THIRTY-ONE SISTERHOOD" was a term coined by our Home Office staff and the Consultants. Many of our Consultants would tell you they love the products, and yes, the income is nice, but they stay for the sisterhood, the connection, and the inclusion. We'd often survey our Consultants and customers about their Thirty-One experience and whenever we asked "What keeps you connected to Thirty-One?" nine times out of ten the answer was "Relationships!" I hear it all the time. Consultants and customers love feeling part of something bigger than themselves.

Consultants who built a team were eventually promoted to the leadership level, which unlocked special perks whenever they shared the opportunity to join our amazing team. Consultants with more than four team members selling our products are promoted to the director level, which enables them to earn extra income, qualify for incentive trips, receive special recognition at our conferences, and hear the latest Thirty-One news before it is shared with the rest of our Consultants. While these are all great perks, many of our leaders really enjoyed the "perks" of supporting their team through their "firsts"—holding their first party, earning their first free product, and receiving their first commission payment. Our leaders found community and connection first and foremost with their teams, which expanded their love for the business even more. These leaders live our mission of women encouraging and empowering other women.

Consultants and leaders who earned incentives by hitting high sales goals felt their connections in our Thirty-One community deepened with every trip and experience. Now, almost twenty years into the business, we've spent time with hundreds, maybe even thousands of Consultants, leaders and families on these trips. These were also special opportunities for our Consultants to celebrate their success with a traveling guest of their choice. Most brought their spouses, but many brought their dads, moms, sisters, or best friends. So many couples would tell stories to Scott and me that these getaways were their first trip without kids, or how they had never taken a honeymoon even though they'd been married for ten-plus years. Together, we celebrated weddings, engagements, and graduations with the Consultants and their loved ones. From time to time, Scott performed wedding ceremonies and vow renewals. Ever since the second incentive trip, there have always been a few "LIT babies" who tagged along with Mom and Dad on subsequent trips. Apparently, the time away proved to be more than just relaxation, spa visits, and pool time for many young couples. Those were such special moments of encouragement and celebration.

On the flip side, we also had opportunities during these celebratory experiences to hear from our Consultants who were going through hard times. It was as much an honor for us when Consultants shared their personal struggles with raising kids, a challenging marriage, or an unwelcomed health diagnosis as it was for us to celebrate their high sales numbers. We wanted our leaders and Consultants to feel celebrated and encouraged in every way, and we truly wanted families and relationships to be better because of Thirty-One.

One of the common themes we heard from spouses, parents, or siblings of our Consultants was how Thirty-One had helped their loved ones build confidence and self-esteem. We believed that encouraging our Consultants with consistent feedback on a monthly, sometimes weekly, basis is what helped them grow into their gifts and pursue their passions. That is why, outside of our in-person times together, we maintained consistent contact, support, and encouragement for our Consultants by providing leadership training webinars, sales-recognition stats, personal and professional development programs, and the latest updates via direct announcements from Scott and me. We created a Facebook community group called "The Pink Bubble" where we shared Consultant recognition, new ideas, and announcements, a tool still used today.

Our web-based intranet for the sales field is called Thirty-One Today. This is where we post training videos; announcements, including those on milestones of achievement for our Consultants; and ways to pull reports to celebrate birthdays and Consultant anniversaries. From time to time, we also send Consultants a fun box in the mail with new products that would arrive (ideally) before any of our customers even had a chance to purchase them. These were all ways we worked hard to encourage our team. And when I say, we worked hard, I mean it. We grew so fast in those first few years that it took a lot of energy and effort to keep encouragement at the forefront of our minds.

In addition to our Facebook group and Thirty-One Today (also known as TOT), we had a weekly "Leader Live" meeting, and I was a regular attendee. Sometimes I showed up to give inspiration; other times I was there to help with big reveals for incentives or new products. We wore St. Patrick's Day hats, pink Gives shirts (more on Gives later), or whatever we could wear to celebrate the particular season. This was our time each week to remind our leaders that we care about them and their businesses.

As Julie describes it so well, the Pink Bubble grew beyond an online social media group:

> The Pink Bubble was how our Consultants described the gatherings of like-minded people who believed in what Thirty-One represented. Whether it was at a team meeting, or in an arena with thousands of people in attendance, the Pink Bubble was a feeling you couldn't avoid.
>
> One of our most unique experiences with Pink Bubble was in 2009 when we hosted our National Conference at Walt Disney World in Orlando, Florida. Thirty-One and Disney World seemed to go hand in hand. The fun-loving culture of both companies made the event a memorable time for our Consultants.
>
> That fun week in Florida also happened to be the week my family was moving to Columbus, so we had a week "away" to transition between our home state to our new state. After Florida, we flew home to Tennessee, hopped in our loaded moving truck, and drove nearly five hundred miles to Ohio for our "this is really happening" move. And the whole time I just kept thinking about how the Pink Bubble made all of this worth the move.

But encouragement didn't mean only the Pink Bubble of connection and communication or the fun surprises for our growing team. It also meant leadership development. One of our in-person training opportunities was Leadership University, which was held a few times a year at our Home Office in Columbus. I was there early so I could greet the one hundred to two hundred leaders and members of the sales and events team as they entered the training room. We would take pictures together, and then I would kick off the meeting by talking about a few of my favorite life themes. These usually included how we are better together and how to be intentional with the people around us—themes that became some of our mantras. I would also ask, "Who do you surround yourself with?" then share my idea of having a life board.

A life board is basically a group of individuals who can counsel you in your personal life, just like most businesses have an advisory board and nonprofits have a board of directors. I encourage our women to think about who they would go to if they needed advice on parenting, marriage, business, health, etc. I'd ask, "Who are those four to eight people who are the phone-a-friend kind of people in your life? The ones you consider your lifelines? These are the people on your 'life board.'" I encouraged the Consultants to write down those names and think of something they could do to make sure each person on that list knew how important they were to them.

The people on my life board list were those I could count on to be honest with me, to tell me the hard things I need to hear, and to celebrate things with me that I didn't normally tell other people. And they *knew* they were on my life board list. Life boards are essential to the encouragement we need as women, business owners, spouses, loved ones, and as CEOs of our own lives.

As you can tell, relationships have always been super important to us. That's why we often told our Consultants and employees that there was so much value in not doing life alone. Scott often quotes a verse from Proverbs 27:17 that says, "As iron sharpens iron, so a friend sharpens a friend" (New Living Translation). And he talks about the fact that, no matter how confident, independent, strong, and courageous we may feel, *we need other people in our lives.* We need others to lift us up and cheer us on, for a shoulder to cry on, to kindly pull our heads out of the clouds, and to allow us the gift of serving others. That's why we were *better together*.

George W. Bush, in his book *41: A Portrait of My Father,* shared a story about asking his mom how she and his dad had such a great marriage. Barbara replied, "Son, we made it because we met each other three-fourths of the way there." What she meant is that their relationship was far more than just meeting each other in the middle. It was about being willing to give more than your "fair share" to the other person in the relationship. That's how Scott and I have had such a great marriage and that's how all of those who joined Thirty-One felt about our organizational culture. We all gave more than our fair share. We were excited about the business and committed to the mission to celebrate, encourage, and reward.

Encouragements were not always warm and fuzzy. We also welcomed those that sounded more like challenges. I always appreciated the employees and Consultants who were willing to challenge me, the ones who resisted going with the flow when they believed strongly in something. Scott says you have to be willing to fight for the things you believe are right. We equally believed in giving in to those whom we respect when we might be wrong. There are different ways we all need to be encouraged and to encourage others.

Scott and I love to be outdoors, hiking, walking, or skiing, so it's easy for us to think about how we interact using outdoor metaphors. At a talk for a National Conference, we spoke about "the Path vs. the Grass." As we go about life, I like to stay on the path, and Scott likes to wander off into the grass. If you haven't figured it out by now, I'm a driven, goal-oriented, work-with-my-head-down kind of gal. I like to know where I'm going and get to it as fast as I can. I see a clear path with an end-goal in mind, and no one has to encourage me to keep moving because I'm on it.

Scott, on the other hand, loves to wander off the path and sit in the grass for a while. He likes to take in all the sights, smells, and details along the way. He appreciates how the flowers are flowing in the breeze and ponders how that rock is still hanging onto the cliff. He pauses to take in deep breaths before he's ready to keep moving along the path. This is a stark contrast to my destination-driven and goal-oriented way. Scott sees life for the journey it is, and I see the destination with some fun and beautiful pit stops along the way.

Neither perspective is wrong. I can appreciate the path, and Scott can appreciate the grass. And we can encourage each other to go at our own speed. This is one way we've realized just how much we need each other, that we truly are better together. Without Scott, I would miss out on so much of life's beauty and wonder. Without me, he may never reach the destination. There have been so many times when I was a little annoyed by his detours, only to discover some of my favorite unexpected experiences during them. I think he would say the same for my pulling, pushing, and nudging. He values the ways I keep him focused on the goal at critical times.

Encouraging each other also takes a lot of curiosity. That's why staying *curious* is one of our values and the topic of a lot of our large-gathering conversations. One of our favorite National Conference speakers, *National Geographic* photographer Dewitt Jones, once told our Consultants, "There's more than one right answer" when it comes to the ways we interact with and encourage each other. Staying curious, even in the hard-driving push of the business, always led us to find unique ways to encourage our team and see what other great organizations were doing. That's why it was important for us to take several of our Home Office team and Consultants through a day at the Disney Institute, or on a tour at the Zappos home office with Lou Fratturo and our kids in tow. Staying curious in the ways we encouraged one another both relationally and professionally is what sparked new ideas for the ways we operated the business. That's why we made it our priority to encourage curiosity and innovation in our teams. We knew that collectively we could discover a better way for just about everything we did when we did it together—because we *are* better together.

We also couldn't possibly talk about the ways we encouraged one another or the ways we were better together without mentioning the close connection between the Thirty-One Consultants and the Home Office. Because we built this business from the ground up, one person at a time, it has always been part of our culture to maintain close face-to-face relationships with our Consultants as our sellers. They are all part of our sisterhood. Our Consultants have always had a direct line to us through our incredible Call Center team for any issues with their independent Thirty-One businesses. In addition to weekly updates, monthly Zoom calls, quarterly Leadership University gatherings, incentive trips, regional product premieres, and our annual National Conference, we frequently arranged training for the Consultants with our Sales and Product teams at the Home Office. Knowing our Consultants by their names and faces was what made our connection with them so encouraging beyond their Thirty-One business.

It wasn't just the leadership team who felt this way, our Home Office staff has always been passionate about connecting with our Consultants. It's been truly remarkable to see how much they've cared for our Consultants and their families over the years. On one incentive trip to Disney, our bus driver said, "How can you *not* love your job when all you see is happy children's smiling faces." And that's how our Home Office team feels about our Consultants.

Now, this kind of connection took some work. It was much more natural for our Call Center reps to develop personal relationships with our Consultants than it was for, say, our warehouse employees.

That's why we would often invite Consultants to the Home Office and warehouse, so they could share their love and appreciation for what all our teams allowed them to do in their businesses. When the warehouse employees could put faces to the people whose businesses they supported, it reinforced that we were all better together. These interactions also made things more encouraging than they might have been otherwise when shipping or product orders got a little, shall we say, "sticky."

A lot of companies will say their business is a relationship business. For some, it's just a façade. But for those of us in the direct sales industry, it's so true. Being "in community" with people you care about is the highest priority, and we're so proud of everyone in the Thirty-One family for living that out all these years. That's why we've prioritized not only celebrating and encouraging one another, but also rewarding our people.

14

REWARD

Recognize Hard Work

THE DIRECT SALES INDUSTRY takes pride in *recognition*. Mary Kay Ash was the queen of recognizing and rewarding people, and in doing so, she set the stage for our entire industry. As usual, we had our own Thirty-One way of showing our Consultants and employees just how much we appreciate and respect them, even before we got to the recognition and rewards.

Our way was rooted in our others-first mentality. This was one of the top reasons people wanted to stay at Thirty-One. Being others-first directed is what helped with retention in the Home Office and with Consultants in the sales field. It's also what allowed our people to show up and do their job better with self-sacrificing (versus ego-driven) attitudes. Our Home Office employees understood that operating with an others-first mentality was the unwritten rule for how we best served our sales field. When we provided a great customer-service experience for our sales field, it resulted in the overall growth of the business. In turn, when Consultants called into or visited the Home Office, they would go above and beyond with expressing their appreciation for the home office team. On various occasions, donuts were delivered to our Call Center team. Handwritten cards and encouraging posters showed up in the mail as a way of saying thank you from our Consultants to our warehouse teams. Showing appreciation was a deeply ingrained part of our culture, and it was a win-win for our sales teams and Home Office. Half the time, our employees and Consultants were rewarding each other before we even had a chance to recognize them.

When we speak of rewards, we sometimes think of trophies, report cards, recognition lists, or other extrinsic motivations that show we are valued or successful in public ways. At Thirty-One, I want people to be publicly recognized for doing well in their roles, but I also want them to feel seen, respected, valued, and successful through intrinsic rewards. That's one of the reasons I have spent hours upon hours making personal phone calls or team conference calls to say hello and share good news with our Consultants. It's why Scott and I have taken thousands of photos with our people. Giving my time is one of the best ways I can personally show appreciation for the many ways they demonstrate dedication and commitment in their own Thirty-One businesses.

We also looked for creative ways to recognize and reward the home office team. Pizza drops during busy seasons were among my favorites. There was nothing like walking into the warehouse with pizza for everyone during an exceptionally busy season. I made it a priority to walk the halls to say hello to our staff and thank them personally. We had an ethnically diverse team, so we hung flags around the top of the warehouse walls to celebrate and honor all the individuals and the countries represented by our team. At one point, there were more than thirty different flags hanging in our Home Office.

Cathy was the first member of our team to start an official "Recognition Department" to acknowledge Consultants for their sales goals, sponsor numbers, and home parties. This team became a vital part of our company, and Cathy and crew helped create, manage, and deliver recognition awards at our annual Leadership Conference (a BIG deal in our company culture), our National Conference, and on our incentive trips throughout the years. Julie pulled reports, Erin and Robbin ordered awards, and Cathy organized the details of recipients for certain awards and when they received them. I was always on hand to reward our team with meaningful recognition and initiate some fun. Calling out names of the celebrated Consultants and employees is a regular highlight for me. Imagine Bob Barker in the good ole' days of *The Price is Right*! This often happened on our monthly leader Zoom calls and when I was traveling town to town. Calling out names of reward recipients at our annual conferences and leadership meetings also meant I got to give lots of hugs as our Consultants and employees came to the stage or warehouse floor. Of course, there were always pictures taken in these moments too. The best part is that the benefits went both ways. Scott and I, along with the Home Office Team, were rewarded with the warm responses of gratitude and love.

Our relationships with our vendors were rewarding too. To celebrate and recognize our vendors at the factories we worked with in China, we would send framed catalogs to hang in their offices. This might not sound like much, but they took such pride in seeing their handmade products presented in our catalogs. On our annual trips with vendors, whether to India or China, we made sure to spend time with the teams of workers to show our appreciation and strengthen relationships. Our visits with these people also helped to build their confidence as they supported us during seasons of fast-paced growth and decline. No matter how much or how little we ordered from them during the last season, their generosity with us on these visits never wavered.

We wondered at times if we sometimes went above and beyond with rewards and recognition in a way that created unhealthy expectations, particularly for our sales field. I remember one sales season in our Ohio office when our Consultants expressed gratitude and, at the same time, had strong opinions about things that didn't go their way. Some even took more than their fair share of the free products offered during our National Conferences. At one point, with more than 10,000 Consultants in attendance at an annual conference, some women were seen hoarding free products by grabbing three or four items from multiple lines around the arena, when everyone was supposed to receive just one new item. I knew what had to happen next: I had to put my foot down and call it out.

During the next general session at that conference, before we revealed more products, I walked on stage and shared a story. I talked about how most of us had experienced the situation where we prepared a Thanksgiving dinner and then worried if we'd made enough mashed potatoes for everyone. It was tradition in the American South to let the kids go through the buffet line first, and sometimes they would take more than their share of the mashed potatoes. When the grown-ups went through the line, they'd be disappointed to find that the mashed potatoes were all gone. I explained that we had a few Consultants who were taking more than their fair share of "mashed potatoes" at the last product giveaway, and that we had ordered only enough for each attendee to have one new product for free. That was my signature Cindy Monroe style of making my point in a way to not offend anyone. And over the years since that talk, I have often been asked about "taking more than your share of the mashed potatoes."

Cathy worked hard to support our Events department by amping up the excitement for incentive trips earned by our Consultants who had top sales numbers each year. The Events team has rewarded all of us with fantastic experiences over the years. For our first incentive trip in 2011, we went to the Moon Palace in Playa del Carmen, Mexico. In 2012, we took 702 people (351 Consultants and their "plus-one") to Cancun. The year after that, it was 986 people in the Dominican Republic, and we worked our way up to an incentive trip to Maui in 2019. The Consultants who earned these trips worked *hard* for these incentives. Their husbands or traveling partners would often come up to Scott and me to thank us for the trip, and our response was always the same: "Don't thank us, thank her!" meaning, thank the Consultant who worked so hard to earn the trip.

Cathy, who played such a big role in supporting these trips, had this to say about them:

> These trips are all about connecting with our Consultants, rewarding their hard-earned accomplishments, and getting to know them on a more personal level. Staying at a beautiful, all-inclusive resort made it easy to spend time with everyone. What's not to love about being at a resort and hanging out with hundreds of your friends? The Home Office team made it a point to take "selfies" with our Consultants as our way of celebrating, rewarding, and remembering their names and faces. This also made it easier for us to build our connections on social media and get to know the Consultants and their families beyond their work with Thirty-One.
>
> Dinner conversations were our favorite. This was time for our team to hear the stories directly from our Consultants and their families about how their lives had been impacted by Thirty-One. I'll never forget the dinner I had on an incentive trip with a Consultant who had been in a horrific car accident months prior to the trip. She had several surgeries and a long recovery. She even had to learn to walk again and lost so much time with her family. But she talked about how supportive her Thirty-One family was during that time, and in the end, she said her journey reminded her that "everyone has a story." It was always an honor when someone shared their story with us. We listened and often prayed with them. To God be the glory!

Cathy and Julie's attention to organization and planning details were what made these trips such a success. Whether it was Riviera Maya, Punta Cana, Atlantis, or Maui, this was such a special time for our Pink Bubble of Consultants and their loved ones. Oftentimes, these trips also signified a promotion along our career path.

These trips included no formal training. It was a lot of pool time, excursions, and maybe a couple of *caipirinhas* (a Brazilian drink). My favorite moments were when we all got to be together for dinner or a group photo. Dinner always included dancing, and many of the trips happened to land on or near my birthday. There is nothing like a birthday party with a thousand of your closest friends! Better than celebrating my birthday, though, was the honor of getting to celebrate all of the hard-working and passionate Consultants who earned the trips. We celebrated those who earned their first trip, those who earned it for the tenth time, and those who earned our "ultra level." Many had joined only a year prior and still earned the trip. While recognition was fun from the stage, it was also fun in the hallways. We celebrated our top earners with sashes on their door, special moments with our Home Office team, and more. One of our favorite special celebrations includes the year we took our ultra-earners to a private island in the Bahamas. As we arrived, we could see pink Thirty-One banners flying everywhere we looked, marking that this was their time and place to be truly celebrated.

I can't forget to mention two incentive trips we had to cancel, both of which happened to be cruises. I got the feeling we are not supposed to cruise at Thirty-One! One trip was canceled at the last minute due to Hurricane Irma in 2017. No one could blame us for not getting on a cruise ship that September week with hurricane winds clocked at 177 miles per hour. The other cancellation happened in 2020 due to COVID-19. We sent awards and amenities to our earners and celebrated their successes the best we could. In 2020, we had a virtual cruise celebration with a family dance party. Yes, our family was on screen dancing to encourage all our earners and their families to dance and celebrate their hard work. We finally had a trip to the Dominican Republic as soon as the world re-opened and we could start traveling again. Talk about a breath of fresh air. The almost three years of not getting together was hard on everyone, which made the celebration of being back together post-COVID even sweeter.

But not all of our celebrations happened during fun and fancy incentive trips. We found small and meaningful ways to celebrate our Consultants in the ways we connected together in-person and online.

Here's how Julie describes those small-scale celebrations:

> Our Celebrate & Connect meetings were on a smaller scale, but many would say they carried a broader impact. These meetings were opportunities for our sales leaders to take the lead and show up for the Consultants on their teams. We provided training content with coordinated topics and even some fun amenities as a way to equip and empower them to develop as well as to celebrate the leaders on their own teams. These gatherings of local team members for an evening or a Saturday of celebration and training occurred on a consistent basis. We encouraged these get togethers because face-to-face connections are a huge part of the success of Thirty-One. The Pink Bubble and the sisterhood couldn't be mistaken during a Celebrate & Connect meeting. We invested an exceptional amount of free products to each attendee at every meeting. But those investments enabled our Consultants to prioritize these events in the midst of everyone's busy schedules.

Other "small" events (if you consider one hundred and fifty Consultants as small) include the gathering of our annual Leadership Council. These were the leaders who earned special recognition to join us on a trip that included updates, training, and the new spring product reveal. This trip usually happened in January to kick off the calendar year. Most leaders loved our trips to the Montage Resort in Laguna Beach, California, the best. That resort, plus the sun and the smell of the sand and the sea, is enough of a celebration for anyone!

Whether it was as simple as a pizza delivery or as posh as an incentive trip to an exotic locale, we decided early on to recognize our people with both extrinsic and intrinsic rewards. And they rewarded us with their love, support, hard work, sales, and the way they gave back to their communities.

15

INVEST

Developing People

AT THE HEIGHT OF OUR GROWTH in 2010–2011, we realized we had invested so heavily in our Consultants with incentive trips, training, marketing resources, and relationship-building that we had outpaced our future with expenses. While many of our competitors were investing in product development—including big-box retailers which carried "knock-offs" of our unique products—we went above and beyond to invest in our people. After all, there's no business quite like the people-oriented direct selling industry. But we spent more on our Consultants than we had budgeted, and as a result, we found ourselves stretched way too thin in other areas at Thirty-One.

In February of 2011, we made the tough decision to do a sponsoring freeze. We struggled with what to do next as we had more orders and Consultants than we could keep up with. We didn't want to keep signing up Consultants and give them a bad experience. I didn't want my name on that, nor did I want our company to be responsible for a bad customer service experience. This meant women who wanted to sign up as new Consultants had to go on a waiting list. Colleagues in our industry warned us that this would be the "kiss of death" for our business model. In just a few months, there were more than 30,000 women on that list. Our Executive Team forecasted numbers and ran projections as we moved these women from the waitlist to the Thirty-One sales field. We purchased huge amounts of inventory for the next season with those 30,000 women in mind.

With new products purchased, we anticipated massive orders by the end of 2011 and the start of 2012. But we didn't take into account how saturated some of our markets would become once our Consultants were hosting parties again among neighborhood friends who were doing the same. Thawing the sponsoring freeze by adding new Consultants didn't have the increased effect on sales we had anticipated. Our Consultant numbers were way up, and so was our excess inventory in the warehouse. The new Consultants were simply not selling and sponsoring at the same rate as the ones who joined before the freeze. We didn't realize the impact that waiting would have on a new Consultant's enthusiasm.

Between the money we spent over our budget on Consultants and the excessive inventory in the warehouse, we had to take a step back and reassess. When we did, we realized we had overextended ourselves with our support to Consultants and our Home Office teams had expanded and become siloed. In an environment where tensions ran high, we had a hard time unifying and owning our mistakes. No one wanted to shoulder the blame.

We had to invest in developing our people in the Home Office if we were ever going to fix our fluctuating number of Consultants and our excess product inventory. This was a trying season for our team. Our values of *accountability* and *flexibility* were constantly working against each other. We didn't always do a good job of holding employees and Consultants accountable. I was afraid of coming off like a b*tch at times, as so many female leaders do. When I anticipated any sort of frustration, I did what I could to avoid conflict and made the fast fix myself. Despite several crucial conversations and new solutions offered, accountability was still difficult. When things got hot, holding people accountable for executing projects on time and within budget was difficult for me.

With massive sales, it was easy to overlook some of the late deadlines, mistakes, and being over budget. But as we began to decline or flatten in sales, those inefficiencies were too costly to the business. I had to start holding people accountable. Difficult conversations were especially challenging when we had people who were hard to manage in the office but were critical to support in the sales field. For that reason, I had a tendency to hang on to people a little too long before letting them go. It also was hard to hold people accountable for executing projects on time and within budget when one of our values was to provide a *gracious* working environment. Holding people accountable and helping them exit the business became more and more necessary and was *always* painful for me.

Then there were individuals who were switched to different positions due to frustrations in their original job or misalignment with their team, and they soared in their new roles. I had to learn what it meant to hold the line and invest in developing people in a way that made the most sense for the business, even when it wasn't what people wanted. This was true for our employees and our Consultants. We couldn't keep bending over backward for our Consultants with compensation packages that simply were not scalable. And we had to start taking things like backorders and airfreight costs into consideration with that compensation. We couldn't keep pumping cash back into the business, so we had to step back and consider our investments carefully.

We decided it was time to invest in the internal team, our facilities, our organizational culture, and what we did day to day around the Thirty-One Home Office. Our team of nearly one thousand employees, including our original crew of friends and the Founding Mothers from Tennessee, had endured more growth than we could ever have imagined as well as eight Home Office/warehouse moves in eight years of business. Whew!

Thankfully, our business was still growing, despite a few setbacks with sponsoring and excess inventory. As a result, our departments and internal teams grew too. This meant we had to get better at clarity, titles, and team responsibilities. So, we hired the right people to boost our Human Resources department. But with a stronger HR presence, including job descriptions, position policies, and team procedures, we started seeing and hearing a pervasive attitude we didn't like. It was one that sounded like "That's not my job!" We had done such a great job of providing clear and thoughtful HR policies and procedures, but what we meant to serve as guidance and guardrails now served as hard and fast rules for many. No longer were our teams willing to function across departments because they were so focused on their own job descriptions. This had to change.

We reminded our employees that HR policies were meant to guide their daily decisions, not guard the exact way they spent their time. We eventually found our way back to functioning as a collaborative team. To do so, we doubled down on our twelve values and started recognizing employees who were living out these values on a daily basis. We acknowledged employees of the month and encouraged collaboration between departments according to these values as often as we could. "All hands on deck" was our motto in that season, as it had been in the early days with such a small founding team.

By this time, everyone also knew that our value of *flexibility* meant to not get too comfortable in their desks, cubes, offices, or roles for too long. We moved so many great people around trying to find the best fit for them and for the company. We moved entire departments from one area of the building to another because they had doubled in size, or because they needed to be closer to another department for collaboration. We added more conference rooms, product rooms, brainstorming areas, training rooms for the Call Center, and we even added a coffee shop for mid-shift refreshments. We spent a lot of time moving, but looking back, I see it was worth it. Those moves almost always translated into greater efficiency and higher productivity, which were necessary to our survival.

We also created an onboarding process for new employees that was, as Julie called it, a masterclass in building community. We definitely had a unique way of sharing the history, vision, mission, values, and culture of Thirty-One that made each new employee connected to our ways. There was always a warm welcome on an employee's first day. That welcome included simple things like smiles and eye contact when being introduced in the hallways. Showing respect in this way was an important and expected aspect of our daily working environment.

I'd be remiss if I didn't mention the amazing leaders we had in that season—leaders like Jon, Lou, and Andrea, who were willing to take on new leadership roles and always rose to the challenge. I'm sure there were other companies nearby paying their employees higher wages with better benefits packages, but we took our responsibility seriously to focus on investing in our internal team, and it paid off. We took care of our people by paying them a competitive wage, developing them as leaders in our company and as individuals outside of their work at Thirty-One. We worked alongside them, recognizing and rewarding them for their contributions to our team. That's what it meant for *all* of us to be "all hands on deck" during a challenging season. We also made a few changes that helped reinforce this mindset:

- We developed an open-door policy with everyone in the Home Office, including the Executive Team. Our doors were opened ninety percent of the time, so people could drop by for purposeful problem solving and casual conversation.
- We started talking and acting like we respected one another and the work being done on other teams. Soon, our hearts followed our actions, and we truly believed in all the reasons we said we respect one another.
- We assigned a finance team member as point person for the various departments in our Home Office and warehouse. This way, every team had direct access to fast solutions for problems that required finances.
- We maximized every opportunity to collaborate across departments and teams. In turn, this pushed out anyone driven by ego to succeed and be above everyone else. By being more about teams than we were about individuals, eventually the people who didn't like this self-selected out and onto something that was a better fit for their goals. This worked in our favor and helped to preserve our company culture.
- We championed an inherent respect for our customers and an others-centered approach for our Consultants. We weren't just pushing products in our Home Office. We were helping people build their lives, thanks to their own small businesses. We were more than our product, and for the first time in a while, we believed it again.

I know I keep saying this, BUT, *relationships* were really the glue to so many pieces of our company along the way, including how we invested in the development of our people. So many of our employees held institutional knowledge about our business as a whole. Once those employees were encouraged and developed to leverage that business knowledge in collaboration with other departments, the relationships they built with their fellow co-workers were just as strong as the relationships they had with our Consultants and sales leaders.

In fact, the greatest cultural shift we made in that season was an internal shift. No longer were we just about the sales field and the Consultants. Now we were also about each other in the Home Office and in the warehouse. This is what contributed to our amazing community and healthy culture, and it's what helped us retain great employees and Consultants for ten-plus years at that point.

Now that we had done the investment work required to develop our Home Office team, we still had to prioritize developing our Consultants. It didn't matter if these Consultants were brand new and just kicking off their businesses with their first party, or if they were seasoned Consultants who were supporting their growing teams of sixteen-plus leaders with hundreds of Consultants under them. Either way, the intentional ways we developed them *mattered.* And we developed this team one person at a time.

Cathy and our Consultant support representatives conducted new Consultant welcome calls on a regular basis. These new Consultants were always happy to hear from someone from the Home Office so soon after they signed up to be part of our company. Cathy also maintained contact with the new Consultants via the New Consultant Facebook page, where she posted celebrations and gave more details about our specials and/or upcoming sales and incentives. She did a lot of live videos for training and encouraged the women to make their own Facebook live videos so their customers could see their personalities come through online. Our teams even took time to write handwritten notes to new and veteran Consultants.

Following Cathy's lead, our sales leaders learned that when they spent quality time getting to know what was important to the Consultants on their team and recognizing their Consultants' accomplishments and kind deeds, this one-on-one focus had an impact on everyone's success. There's a saying we'd often share with our sales leaders as we worked to develop them: "A team member will quit on a boss, but not a friend" (author unknown). Another of my favorite sayings is based on a quote from Theodore Roosevelt — "Your team doesn't care how much you know; they care about how much you care." That's why we made storytelling part of our developmental culture. We always ask Consultants to share their stories at retreats or monthly meetings. Hearing these individual stories enables others to build their own confidence. It gives them something to identify with and makes running their own business feel attainable when they see it played out through someone else's life.

Developing people became equally important for me in my personal life. I struggled to connect with friends and family outside of Thirty-One because my life was my work. Then I read about the number of true friends the average adult has over their lifetime. There have been multiple studies on this, but most say that the average adult only has three to five close personal relationships that last for life. That refers to those whom you know you can count on or friends who maintain a consistent connection. Scott had those kinds of friends, but outside of my Thirty-One friends, I had to think about the number of "true friends" I had.

Because I'm always in entrepreneurial mode, I also started to think about, if those statistics were accurate, what kind of impact we could have at our Thirty-One parties by providing the opportunity for women to meet new friends or reunite with old ones. We could literally change those statistics by focusing on friendships, something we did well in the beginning. It was something that needed more of our focus. Reading that article reignited my own pursuit of friends outside of the business.

I found fun ways to invest in my relationships by setting consistent lunch dates with Janet and making time for monthly Zooms with my dear friend Andrea. Amy and I would often meet up for dinner or happy hour, and I still jump at any chance I get to hop on an airplane and visit my friend Joan. Investing in these friendships required me to say no to some of the other investments I was making in my life, personally and professionally. I opted out of meetings with my team or gave up a night at home watching my favorite TV series with Scott, or I put a hold on reading that book on my nightstand to make room for investing in friends. The rewards I get from making those investments, as well as making investments in our employees and our Consultants, bring so much value and joy to my life.

Here's what I know to be true: Investing in relationships is critical to our personal growth as people, just as investing in business is critical to the continued growth and success of our company. Scott and I have experienced highs and lows as we've made sacrifices to make investments in all areas of our lives. And we've seen both wins and losses in investments across our timeline and history at Thirty-One. If there's one thing we've learned along the way, it's that the most rewarding investments aren't something you can track on paper or in a spreadsheet, but I believe they offer the most rewarding return on investment. That's why investing in the development of others wasn't just a priority we made for a particular season at Thirty-One. It was a commitment we made for the long haul.

16

COMMIT

Deep Roots

DURING THE TIME SPENT focusing on how to invest in the development of relationships, I had forgotten an important investment. I needed to invest in ME. If I was going to stay in this business for the long haul, I needed to look after myself. Keeping the commitments we made to our business required digging deep for energy and answers, and I couldn't do it on my own. I had to reach out to find the right tools, and one of those tools was a business coach.

In the first ten years of rapid business growth, the hours were long, but the ride was fun, and the momentum kept us going. I did not have much time to attend outside leadership events and retreats or to develop myself outside of reading books. I had been told about great CEO organizations and mastermind groups I could join, but I never considered it because I was focused on Thirty-One. If there was any place I felt needed more of my time, it was at home with my family.

After the business began to shift from growth to declining and flattening sales numbers, I needed to work on the business in a different way. It had been all-consuming, and I was reacting in the moment rather than being strategic with a long-term plan in mind. This side of leadership was definitely not as much fun and it became exhausting. I didn't have many people to talk to about turning the business back toward growth again or about dealing with the exhaustion. I had supportive team members, amazing friends, a wonderful husband and kids, and an advisory board for feedback, advice, and resources, but I was stuck and needed something or someone else to help me dig deep.

Several people mentioned an organization called the Young Presidents Organization (YPO). It was an elite group of presidents and CEOs who were running businesses of significant size. I had a sense YPO was where I would find the help I needed, so I joined and immediately became involved.

A few weeks later, on my first retreat with a small group of YPO leaders, I found myself sharing all my fears and feelings with strangers. They not only seemed to care, but they also understood what I was saying and didn't judge me for my declining business or for the tearful emotions attached to this chapter of my career. The facilitator for our group retreat was a man named Craig Wiley. He was kind and thoughtful and created such a safe space for us to show up and share our full and vulnerable selves. Craig was an executive coach for business owners like me, so I reached out to see if he would coach me. I told him I needed help to get unstuck from being a "hot mess" of a leader. Sure enough, Craig was up for the challenge.

We began meeting every other week over the phone. I wasn't depressed or anxious, although I was perhaps a little embarrassed by our sales decline. The word I used over and over in our conversations was "exhausted." I kept telling Craig how exhausted I was, even after getting plenty of sleep. It was emotional exhaustion from being stuck, leading without confidence, and suffering frustration from not being able to figure out how to move us back toward growth.

It took a few months of coaching with Craig to feel like I was beginning to find myself and my confidence again. Craig helped me get unstuck and focus on what I knew to be true about the business, our customers, and our Consultants. I was ready to share tools I had learned with my team. One of the practical things he taught me was to leave space in Executive Team planning meetings to make real-time decisions, even if they altered our strategic plans. This meant operating out of real-time strategies and, over six to nine months, this new method of operating began to work. Our Consultants were back producing millions of dollars in sales, which flattened the curve of our numbers and right sized our business. Things were looking much better.

While I was feeling more in control of my role in the business and like I had started to establish certain rhythms, our Home Office team and sales leaders were still struggling and tired. I could see exhaustion in their eyes, the same exhaustion I talked to Craig about for months on end. So, I hired Craig and his team to help us in re-envisioning how we worked together and collaborated on solutions and systems.

Cathy recalled a turning point for the team when Craig had them share their personal journeys. This was who Craig was. He wanted our team to grow toward better business results, but he cared about who we all are in the process. Craig and his team helped our sales team work better together and collaborate on solutions for the visions they had. As a result, they began to build greater trust and succeed in new and different ways.

Craig and I created coaching content for our Consultants, and in 2016, we offered a Leadership Summit retreat for our sales leaders. The goal of the summit was to teach our leaders some of the same solutions-oriented ways of thinking I learned with Craig. Over the years, I have learned that we all use different tools to find renewal and confidence. There's no one-size-fits-all solution. I'm happy to say that many of those leaders walked away from that weekend with confidence and fresh thinking about their business from the tools we shared. Others gained deeper relationships and renewed confidence in their Thirty-One community.

Through my personal time of growth, one of the habits I established was to carry a small notebook with me. I jotted down my favorite quotes and takeaways from books, advisors, and conferences. I kept thoughts that were most relevant to me and others in our business. I was always reading the next leadership or self-help book to navigate each new phase of our business and life. Learning was how I dug deep and leaned into my potential.

We also kept a library of my favorite books in the Home Office. I would use them as resources for conference talks and leadership training with our sales field, and I shared them with our staff. I would remind our teams and leaders of how to stay focused by putting our actions toward activities that helped us reach our goals. This included filtering what we read and being strategic about how we spent our time. I was often asked, "What book are you reading right now?" People knew this was the best way to get my attention, hear about my latest passion, and understand where my mind was at the time.

During our Leadership University conference in 2016, Hurricane Matthew had just blown through the South. Before delivering the opening talk of our session one day, I watched videos on the morning news of tall trees being blown so hard they were lying down, bent over against the ground. Their deep roots were the only thing keeping those trees intact. After the hurricane blew through the area, most of the trees stood back up straight and tall. With sunshine and time, they were strong enough to produce new growth. It struck me that *THIS* was the metaphor for my life and our business in that season. I had survived the hurricane of overextending our business finances with generous compensation plans, excess stock-piles in our warehouse, and declining sales. But my roots ran deep, and so did the roots of Thirty-One, thanks to the company culture we had built. So, I asked the leaders attending the meeting about their commitments, their roots, and their intended growth for their business, family, and faith.

As I shared this metaphor and challenge, Carolyn, one of our leaders from Canada, shared an exercise she did every morning. She would stand, feeling her feet on the floor, and imagine her feet taking roots that went down into the floor. Then she asked herself, "What's taking root in your day today?" What a great exercise to reinforce the metaphor! I closed our session that day by encouraging all of the Consultants in the room to consider: "What are you committing to today as you develop deep roots in your leadership journey? What does this journey mean to you? How does it make you feel?" I chose to plant my feet and grow deep roots into my faith, my family, and Thirty-One. I hoped and prayed they chose to do the same.

Being deeply rooted in what I believe in and am passionate about has allowed me to survive and succeed in my business. But it's also enabled me to make a strong commitment to a life of joy and contentment despite the occasional "hurricane" situation and season. After all, I believe every woman deserves to live the life she loves. And that's the commitment I made to *me*.

17

GIVE

Live Generously

EACH HOLIDAY SEASON from 2009–2018, we had the opportunity to give Thirty-One products away through *The Today Show*'s annual toy drive to Boys and Girls Clubs across the country. Some of our Consultants participated in the distribution to kids in their local communities, and we all were blessed to be part of such significant generosity. For many years, we were recognized by *Today* as one of the top donors of the drive. Most years, I was invited to appear on the show and share the Thirty-One story and the products we were donating.

While it might seem exciting to get my hair and makeup done by professional TV crews and hang out in the green room with news celebrities, I was a hot mess. Armpit sweat, butterflies, and frequent visits to the bathroom (like ten times in the hour I was backstage waiting). Live national TV was pressure enough on its own, but I was just as nervous about representing the thirty-plus Consultants who flew into New York City to join in the fun by standing outside the *Today* studios in the freezing cold and, in some years, rain. These women would wake up in their nearby hotel rooms at 4:30 a.m., put on their pink Santa hats, show up with their Thirty-One cheer signs, and celebrate our opportunity to give back in big ways . . . and maybe meet Al Roker! This was such a special season, and it warmed my heart to see the spirit of generosity spread like wildfire with our team.

While the company was growing and my time was spent chasing the ball downhill, I wanted to create a culture of giving. It was hard to prioritize philanthropic activities and partnerships when we were engaged in challenges on a daily basis, but I didn't want us to lose our spirit of generosity. So we created a full-time role to support our philanthropic efforts and hired Wendy Bradshaw to be our generosity champion. I worked alongside Wendy, who was much loved by our Home Office team and sales field, to set up three pillars of serving as a guide for any donation requests and our Thirty-One Gives strategy. These three pillars are Women, Girls, and Family, and each of our endeavors through Gives supports at least one of them.

Our local Thirty-One family had been supporting the Ronald McDonald House in Columbus before we expanded the partnership to the national level. Our employees and Consultants served meals at Ronald McDonald Houses across the country. We also supported the Girls on the Run race in Columbus, which also led to a partnership with their international organization.

Our hearts were constantly filled with love and gratitude for opportunities to give back as a company, but the blessing of seeing our Consultants invest their time and gifts directly into their communities across the United States and Canada was mind-blowing. The countless communities where our teams showed up, gave, and served were strengthened in such special ways. According to Cathy, Thirty-One Gives was the heartbeat of our company.

Here are some of Cathy and Julie's favorite memories from Thirty-One Gives:

JULIE:

We started Thirty-One Gives in February 2012 with a focus on empowering women and girls. It was how we decided to give back to the communities we lived in. We did this because we believe confident girls become strong women who lead healthy families and build thriving communities. That is the vision for Thirty-One Gives. In 2012, we had over 90,000 Consultants who were generously ready to give. Little did we know what an impact our Consultants would have in the coming years. At the time of this printing, Thirty-One has facilitated the donations of more than $183 million in products and cash to charitable organizations who share our vision of thriving communities built by confident girls and strong women. A few of those organizations were Girls on the Run, the Salvation Army, the Ronald McDonald House, and nonprofits providing disaster relief for national weather-related disasters.

For the **SALVATION ARMY CHRISTMAS TOY DRIVE**, we gathered new, unwrapped toy donations from our employees and offered work shifts for them to join us at the Salvation Army facility before Christmas. People in greatest need were able to come by and "shop" for gifts for their families and leave with a box full of holiday meal items so their family could have a wonderful holiday. Over the years, Thirty-One has donated more than 100,000 products worth over $4 million to the Salvation Army through Thirty-One Gives.

The **RONALD MCDONALD HOUSE (RMH)** was one of our longest standing partnerships with a national charitable organization. It included the donation of free totes monogrammed with the RMH logo so families could carry their personal items to and from the hospital. In eight years, we donated more than 900,000 products worth over $33 million to build care bags for families staying at Ronald McDonald Houses. Another way we served RMH was, on the 31st of every month, our teams in both Ohio and Tennessee served meals to families staying at the houses. We planned the menu, brought food and supplies, and cooked and prepped the meals. We loved all serving together.

DISASTER RELIEF was another area where we stepped up. Countless times we heard about towns where some of our Consultants lived that were impacted by severe storms, hurricanes, or tornadoes. To support relief efforts, we donated more than 1.6 million products worth over $39 million to World Vision. Most of these products were used to build care packages for local disaster relief areas. This was truly the heart of Thirty-One Gives.

CATHY:

GIRLS ON THE RUN (GOTR) is an international nonprofit organization with a mission to "inspire girls to be joyful, healthy, and confident using a fun, experience-based curriculum which creatively integrates running." GOTR puts emphasis on developing confidence, character, caring, and connection through running and other physical activities with girls in third through eighth grades. We were fortunate enough to sponsor several of the local GOTR events and 5K celebrations happening in and around Columbus. We'd stand on the sidelines of these races to cheer them on with our signature pink pom-poms, homemade signs, clappers, loud voices, and big smiles. After these events, we handed out products and talked to the girls about how the GOTR program helped them. They would smile and say that they had more confidence, made new friends, and learned to persevere in many things in their lives as a result of the program. When we first began supporting GOTR, they had already reached one million girls with their positive message. Between 2016 and 2022, we helped Girls on the Run reach an additional one million girls. Since 2016, Thirty-One Gives has helped facilitate the donation of more than $17 million in products and cash to Girls on the Run. In 2021 alone, Thirty-One Gives raised $1.8M in product and cash donations to benefit Girls on the Run.

During several holiday seasons, dozens of our Home Office team members partnered with the **SALVATION ARMY** as bell-ringers at the local mall. Sounds like an easy way to give back but sitting outside on a cold winter day in Ohio was a difficult job for us Southern gals who had moved from Tennessee. I still remember the first time I signed up to ring the bell. Thank goodness I bundled up with extra layers and ALL my warm clothes. In the end, we were all thankful for the opportunity to volunteer and do our part.

To celebrate the fifteenth anniversary of Thirty-One, we funded a kids' playroom makeover at the **RONALD MCDONALD HOUSE** in Chattanooga. That was one of my favorite projects. We collaborated with RMH staff, a few of our Consultants and Home Office employees, a contractor, and a design blogger to upgrade this space in every way. There's still a plaque hanging on the playroom wall that reads: "Proudly presented to the families at the Ronald McDonald House Chattanooga to commemorate the 15th Anniversary of Thirty-One Gifts founded in Chattanooga by Cindy Monroe and employees Julie Sutton, Cathy Smith and Laura Smith and Independent Sales Consultants Jenny Hillenburg, Holley Cox and Dawn Brown." This plaque makes us so PROUD every time we walk by and see it.

Thankfully, our sales field, including our Consultants and leaders, loved to give back by sharing about the organizations we supported through Thirty-One Gives. They also loved to support organizations that were close to their own hearts—organizations in their local communities or the nonprofits they started due to their own areas of passion and need.

To sustain and grow our philanthropic efforts, we created the Gives Care Council, composed of ten Consultants from the United States and Canada. These Consultants serve as the voice for Thirty-One regarding Thirty-One Gives and its mission. Every year we ask our sales field to nominate one of their peers who goes above and beyond to carry out our vision of giving at Thirty-One. In 2013, the Council established the Thirty-One Gives "Heart of Her Award." This award was created to honor a Thirty-One leader who exemplifies the essence of Gives by offering her time, talent, and treasure to support philanthropic work in her local community while upholding the characteristics of a virtuous woman and balancing a successful business with Thirty-One. A team from the Home Office reviews and narrows them down to three to five nominations to give to me. I select one Consultant each year to receive this special award. What a difficult decision! But what a blessing these women and their stories have been to me over the years. Some of my most emotional memories have been the moments we get to award and celebrate these ladies and the impact they are having beyond their businesses.

Another holiday giving event that many of our Consultants support each season is the Samaritan's Purse Operation Christmas Child (OCC). While this was not an official organization supported by Gives, our Thirty-One family loved their mission. Scott's mother, Ger, had been saving and buying for her Operation Christmas Child boxes for as long as I'd known her. So, when one of our Heart of Her stories was about OCC, I was beaming. I posted on social media about our family's love for OCC, and soon after, Scott, Alyx, Evan, and I were invited to go on a delivery trip in Guyana with the Samaritan's Purse team. We jumped at the opportunity to go as a family and deliver boxes and share God's love. It was a family highlight for us that reinforced our Gives mission in a different way.

Thinking about these Christmas boxes reminds me of another philanthropic opportunity we offered at our National Conference. One year, Wendy mentioned World Vision as a partner of Thirty-One during a season of heavy disaster relief here in the United States. The team at World Vision loved partnering with us to build what they called Hope Kits. So that year at our annual conference, we created a special time with our Senior Consultants to create Hope Kits with our Thirty-One beauty bags. We had pallets of shampoo, soap, toothbrushes, and personal hygiene items to fill these bags. There was an assembly line to put the products in each bag, and at the end of the line was an area for us to write handwritten notes to include in each bag as our way to send love to a woman receiving the bag. So many of our husbands and family members in attendance that year worked on setting up and making sure things ran smoothly for the kit assembly lines. To complete this circle of love, there were times when World Vision partnered with Thirty-One Gives in New York City to give these Hope Kits to women through the YWCA or women's shelters. The impact we had was significant, but we never grew tired of these amazing opportunities to give.

Here's how Julie described the influence we had as a company through our Consultants in the sales field:

> Our Consultants had a gift for using their influence for good. We saw proof of this when our Consultants were inspired by what we did at the Home Office through our Thirty-One Gives philanthropic arm, and they took it to another level. Whether we changed our charitable partners on a quarterly basis or partnered with them for a longer-term arrangement, our Consultants loved learning about these partners. Together, we facilitated donations of more than $183 million to benefit the charities we believed in as a company. Many of our Consultants maintained relationships with these charities for years beyond our initial support. They would also go on to create additional give-back opportunities, fundraisers, and giveaways with charities all on their own.
>
> We still hear stories on a regular basis of the impact our Consultants made through their charitable giving and creative ideas. One story was a "chemo care bag" fundraiser. A few of our Consultants asked their customers to contribute a small amount toward a give-back opportunity. In turn they created Thirty-One bags filled with necessities someone would appreciate while going through chemotherapy. Chemo care bags were given in bulk to a hospital in their home area. The patients who received these items shared amazing stories of how those bags made their days a little easier. Stories like this were over and above what we encouraged our Consultants to do. They did it anyway, with the passion of real Proverbs 31 women.

We have had so many great moments of giving throughout our years as a company. As I celebrate the moments, the memories, and the number of lives who have been blessed, I know that we couldn't have done it without Wendy Bradshaw, The Gives Care Council, our Home Office team, and all of the Consultants in our sales field who organized and showed up to reach our giving potential as a collective body of people who love to give. We've been blessed to the point of overflowing, and we are so happy to live big and give generously through Thirty-One Gives.

18

REACH

Lean into Your Potential

MARY KAY ASH, a direct sales icon, was one of my biggest role models. I read in her book that most people only reach ten percent of their potential in a lifetime. This stark reality of most people missing out on ninety percent of their capabilities deeply moved me, and I took it as a personal challenge to encourage and empower a generation of women to live out more of their potential.

I once told our Consultants, "My dream isn't to build a direct selling empire, be in magazines, or wind up at the top of a 'Who's Who' list. My greatest dream is to help as many women as I can to tap into their unused potential. That's what gets me out of bed every morning. None of us should get to the end of our lives having reached only ten percent of our potential. Our world needs me, you, and every single one of us to reach our potential." I was so proud every time one of our Consultants turned a simple $99 enrollment kit into the business of their dreams. In an unending ripple effect, they then inspired and empowered their families, friends, and communities to reach their potential. I know because I heard their stories in person, or read them in e-mails and online posts.

Here's the secret about reaching our full potential: We can't do it on our own. I know, I know. How could those words be coming from me? Those who know me well know I'm a very independent person. And in today's world, it's popular to believe that a strong, independent person makes things happen on her own. My own knee-jerk reaction was to try making things happen on my own. It wasn't until I started writing this book that I could connect the dots between how much of that reaction was formed the night a spark lit my childhood home on fire. Early life experiences have a funny way of subconsciously shaping us for the rest of our lives. Feeling as though I was all alone that night, the only one looking out for me, still drives my fierce sense of independence. But I believe God surrounds us with amazing people who can add value to our lives, and we can add value to their lives.

As the business grew, declined, flattened, then grew again, we did our best to surround ourselves with amazing people and expert talent. This is true in any thriving business, but I'd like to think it was *especially* true in ours. There are so many people we could talk and write about. Julie remembers two particularly amazing individuals with expert talent:

> Because the company culture at Thirty-One has been exceptionally open and warm, it was not uncommon for someone to start working in one role only to find their personality or skills were a better fit in a different role in a different department. And this was okay! We've always been the kind of business where everyone feels like they're part of something bigger, where they sense they are making a bigger impact beyond their own capabilities.
>
> **ERIN WELCH,** one of our Founding Mothers, began with us in a utility role where anything and everything could be thrown her way before she found a fitting role managing our Career and Guidelines Support department. This department handled the Consultant complexities of being independent sales reps where there were specific policies and procedures to follow. The complicated part of our

> Consultants not being employees of Thirty-One meant that we had to toe a fine line when it came to issues that arose with their performance or leadership. Erin knew the ins and outs of the commission structure and the leadership career path. When the time was right, she moved into a Recognition role for our sales field. Her heart was focused on celebrating, encouraging, and rewarding our Consultants, and they felt the love.
>
> **BRIAN MATNEY** is another example of someone who stepped up to a level of performance that was far beyond why he was originally hired at Thirty-One. Brian started in our Merchandise Planning department and was deeply involved daily in spreadsheets of inventory metrics and product performance data. After five years with the company, Brian moved into a strategic planning role in which he influenced overall company initiatives and sales field programs and incentives. He's been with the company for more than ten years.

We could go on and on.

Whenever we found amazing people with expert talent in and around Thirty-One, I also had to be mindful not to leverage those people only to help us achieve our own goals and success. Yes, those people helped us lean into our potential, but that didn't always translate directly to our bottom line of success. Sometimes it translated to the slow transformation of an idea, an individual, or a long-term decision. That's why I have always tried to encourage our sales field to not "use" their customers and their team of Consultants to help them earn that big incentive trip. Instead, they needed to stay focused on the gift of those relationships and to love their people well. We have a human tendency to get laser-focused when something big is at stake, even if it means we have to roll over people in the process. The reality is that most people can see right through it when we operate that way. In my experience, using a friend to achieve a personal goal without her best interest in mind never ends well. The big "carrot" dangling at the end of whatever stick you're holding is never worth misaligned motives, a lack of trust, or damage to a relationship. And it's definitely not how we lean into our full potential.

At Thirty-One, one of our overarching goals, besides encouraging and empowering women, was to build a community of trust, authenticity, and open sharing. This was how we reached for our fullest potential, and it's the reason *authenticity* is one of our twelve core values. We also believe strongly that we were created by God to live together in real community. Not because living in community always felt like it worked in our favor, but because it seemed like the right way to live according to the story of God and God's people as told throughout the Bible.

Part of building this strong, authentic, and connected community meant including our Consultants and sales field leaders in the changes we made as we moved forward. We found ways to pull our leaders in for their input and feedback. This wasn't always easy, believe me. But it was the best thing we could do to reach for our full potential while also encouraging these women to reach their full potential.

Truth was, our Consultants were our No. 1 customers. They were also our No. 1 critics. If we could harness their critiques for good, they felt seen and heard, and we had valuable input that shaped our next season of product orders and strategic decisions. To gather this feedback, we developed a small group called the Presidential Advisory Council of our top sales leaders around the country. This led to a bigger group of sales leaders called the Leadership Council, and another group called the Gives Care Council. Some of these leaders gave input during the development phase of our products, our strategic growth initiatives, and regarding marketing tools such as our social media presence and catalogs. Others gave feedback on how we could lean into our potential by making a bigger impact in the community through our charitable department, Thirty-One Gives. Most of the time, we were relying on these women to help us promote new products and ideas, communicate updates and changes, and be our ambassadors to the rest of the Consultants in our sales field.

The most fabulous thing about these councils was that I got to know many of our leaders really well. They became the kind of friends who had my back—the text-me-at-midnight kind of having my back. If something wasn't going well with our products or our Consultants, our leaders were on the front lines and knew the details before our Home Office team usually did. They had solutions before we even knew about the problems. If things were going well, my phone was silent, which was a good thing. There were times when their feedback didn't match the data or the forecasted trends. But the "soft" data provided by these council leaders helped us make the best decisions possible in real time. Earning a seat on one of our councils was an exclusive recognition for our top leaders, and it meant one-on-one quality time with our Home Office team. These councils were a viable part of growing our business, but the relationships were the goldmine we discovered. The insights we had a result of their input outweighed any struggles with the balance between listening too much and not listening enough. Over time, these councils brought out the best in all of us, just as we had hoped they would do.

Looking back now, I can see how the start of these councils was a crucial moment for our team, both inside the office and outside in sales. When we built Thirty-One, we were determined to be transparent and honest with our field. But fast growth meant things got missed and updates were old news before they even made it to every level of our team. There wasn't always a chance to be transparent about every single decision with our Consultants, but we could be authentic in the way we conducted our business and updated everyone. We were always going back to the notion of *authenticity* as one of our company values. When we brainstormed new marketing ideas, we'd step back and ask, "Is this idea authentic to who we are and the way we show up in the world?" Every time Scott and I prepared a talk for Leadership University, a council meeting, or a conference, we asked each other, "Does this sound authentic to us?" If it did, we kept it. If it didn't, we reworked things until it did. We never wanted to be the kind of company that rolled out a marketing package full of empty promises, which would have been easy to do.

There are a few not-so-flattering reputations in the direct sales industry that are the exact opposite of what it meant for us to lean into our potential. One of them is a reputation of stretching the truth about product benefits or compensation claims. We worked day and night against that reputation. We are committed to being real and authentic in every way possible, professionally, and personally.

Another not-so-flattering reputation in direct sales is the game of competition and comparison. After twenty-plus years in the business, including my short stint selling kitchenware prior to Thirty-One, I've watched a lot of people in direct selling who were always trying to be like someone else, constantly comparing themselves to others. But comparison can be a dangerous trap. Trying to fit into someone else's mold is painful for the person doing it and painful for those with a front row seat to watch it unfold. Thankfully, comparison hasn't been a vice or a dangerous trap for me; it's just not the way I'm wired. I've known my whole life that I wanted to be me, albeit there have been seasons when I've wanted to be a *better* version of me.

I haven't always been confident in my own abilities, but I have always been sure that I wanted only to be the best version of the person God made me to be. I've had plenty of struggles, but I am a what-you-see-is-what-you-get kind of person. Sometimes that gets me in trouble because I have a tendency to say whatever is on my mind, but overall, the idea of being authentic has played to my favor. You always know where you stand with me, and you can trust my intentions. We wanted our company to have that kind of honest and authentic reputation too.

It was hard to be a Thirty-One Consultant if you weren't willing to be authentic. We built a culture around being yourself. Those who couldn't show up and be themselves were the Consultants who didn't feel like they belonged, and we wanted everyone to belong. But we needed our team to be willing to lean into our values to reach their fullest potential with us. Whenever we talked about this idea of belonging and being yourself at conferences or councils, Scott would quote Oscar Wilde, who once said, "Be yourself because everyone else is taken." There are so many of us walking around with low self-confidence and self-esteem, and if those issues aren't addressed at some point, they keep us from being ourselves. But as I've watched Consultants learn to lean into their own potential and leverage their own voices and ideas, I've seen their miraculous transformative growth.

I once got up on a conference stage and said to almost 15,000 Consultants staring back at me, "I didn't create Thirty-One for me. I created Thirty-One so you would find you." I meant every word of it. I was always hearing about women who were quiet and shy and hid behind their household responsibilities, but once they discovered their potential with our business, they outpaced the CEO-moms selling Thirty-One products a few blocks over. We may have provided the opportunity, products, and tools, but those women learned to lean into their own potential to be extraordinary.

In the process of building our business and building our lives, we realized that authenticity and the ability to reach our fullest potential often go hand in hand. When we are truly our authentic selves, people trust us and believe in us and do whatever they can to help us succeed. I believed this for our women as they joined our team, and I believe this for anyone reading this book right now. You already have what it takes to lean into your fullest potential. You just need to be you.

19

INFLUENCE

Use What You Have

IN 2015, I was named to the *Forbes Magazine* list of "Self-Made Women to Watch." I had just turned forty, and there I was on a magazine page between Taylor Swift and Sandra Bullock. There were eight of us, each with our own full-color photo in one of the most renowned magazines. I made my living off of encouraging women and selling pretty bags. The other seven women made their living making award-winning music and blockbuster movies. I was humbled, to say the least. And I was *really uncomfortable.*

I worried about the impact of the article. I wanted it to encourage girls and women to consider becoming entrepreneurs, to take risks and build businesses of their own. But I was worried my Consultants thought I was getting "too big for my britches." I didn't want them to put me on an unapproachable pedestal. What most of them didn't know was that I wasn't off stashing cash from the business in my personal accounts. Scott and I were pouring much of the profits back into the business. Things were looking up after our sponsor freeze and excess inventory situation, but we were still "all hands on deck" with climbing out of that season.

Being in the limelight made me nervous, no matter how many times it happened. Anytime I was interviewed for a TV news spot or onstage at our Direct Selling Association meetings, I had sweaty palms, butterflies in my stomach, and a shaky voice. I was comfortable standing in front of thousands of Consultants at our annual Thirty-One conferences, but outside speaking engagements were different.

At conferences, I usually had notes in hand or a teleprompter with a script I had written ahead of time. Interviews, on the other hand, were spontaneous, and I had to "fly by the seat of my pants," which is not typically my style. I liked to take risks, but they were usually calculated risks. When someone else facilitated a live conversation with many other people watching, I felt vulnerable. I worried they would discover that I wasn't an experienced CEO or that I used the wrong pronunciation of a word. I wanted to know what questions they were going to ask so I'd have the right things to say at the right times. Still, nine times out of ten, those unscripted interviews went over just fine. On occasion, I wished I had a chance for a redo, but that's not how those thing work. I just needed to keep moving on. Interviews for magazine articles were similar. I felt like I was putting myself out there for the world to see and feared I might not meet their expectations and measure up as a female entrepreneur and CEO.

I didn't have control over every article or interview, but these experiences made me want to be *thoughtful* when opportunities *were* in my control. Whenever I was asked to do a speaking engagement, I used the same four personal filters to decide if I would say yes:

1. I asked about the audience. How many people would be in attendance, meaning how many people would I have the opportunity to impact?
2. I'd ask about the theme or topic and how they saw my

story relating to it. Was it about our business or my story that made them ask me for this particular topic?

3. I'd ask about time. How much time was this going to require my being away from my family and my business?
4. I asked about the opportunity. What were the details and logistics?

I got into such a consistent rhythm of fielding these requests with these questions that I asked my assistant to create a document with four big corresponding squares on it so I could jot down the details when these requests came in. I wanted to make sure that my story would be encouraging and impactful, but also the best use of my time. I appreciated the opportunity to exercise my influence in this way, but I wanted to use what I already had without stealing essential time from the places where I had the most impact: at home and at Thirty-One. Because speaking was not the most comfortable thing for me to do, if I was going to put myself out there, I wanted it to be with purpose.

I've shared my thoughts about making an *impact,* but as I think about *influence,* it feels a different than impact. Making an impact is forward momentum, but using my influence is more passive or receptive energy. It's less active and, truthfully, I have less control. My guess is that most of my influence happens with people who are watching my life from a distance. But most of my impact happens with people in my daily relationships. Both can have a ripple effect, and both require some kind of leadership and action. Using my influence is less tangible; it's hard to measure. And we all know by now how much I like to measure things—*growth, strategy, risk, fun,* you name it. When it comes to using my influence, I've had to remind myself to use what I have. As long as I was authentic and true to my purpose and goals, and as long as my influence was positive, then measuring the size of my influence didn't matter. My best guess based on my own experience is that most of our influence is way more exponential than we could ever imagine.

About the time I turned forty and hit the *Forbes* list, I realized there were patterns to the way my influence had expanded beyond my family, friends, and team, even well-beyond Thirty-One. The greatest area where I could see this pattern was in my relationships. If you're sensing a theme that relationships were vital to every area of my life, you're right. I have always wanted people to follow my leadership out of trust and respect. This meant I had to be genuine and real. I've also wanted people to find ways to lead *with* me. That's the kind of influence I want to be known for. I want to be the leader who encourages and empowers others to lead. That's why sharing stories has been such an important part of our company culture. In the Home Office, departments were encouraged to have lunch together or grab drinks after work and spend time sharing their stories. This was all to encourage relationship-building, trust, authenticity, and influence. I wanted our leaders, Consultants, and teams to see that we never run out of opportunities to influence other people. That is the key to business and life.

We often heard stories about how meaningful the random phone calls and text exchanges between Consultants and employees or Consultants and Consultants were. Cathy shares a story about the time she couldn't get one of our Consultants off her mind. She sent a quick text saying, "Hi, just checking in to make sure you are doing okay. God put you on my heart today, so I knew I needed to reach out." The Consultant replied that Cathy's text was perfect timing and what she needed in the moment. We heard this kind of story all the time.

It was just as important for all of us at Thirty-One to realize who we were allowing to influence our lives. A significant majority of our Consultants have been married women between the ages of thirty and forty-five years old, although we have had some older and younger women, single women, and even a few men. As is typical in our industry, most often it was a wife working as a Consultant. Many of the husbands admitted they were skeptical of this "thing" their wives had joined. If a spouse wasn't supportive, we watched how our Consultants struggled to have confidence in their role as independent business owners. It was amazing to see how much influence these men had over their wives' businesses, even if they weren't involved, and at times, *especially* because they weren't involved. That was never my experience with Scott. He's always been such a hugely positive influence from the start of my business. It's also why we made it a point to have a class for HOTs (husbands of Thirty-One) at every conference.

Scott talked a lot about influence in those conversations. It's been a remarkable blessing to see how much influence they had on changing the perspective of the spouses. The married couples in attendance learned that they both had so much influence over whether the other felt loved and supported. The husbands or partners had influence over their loved ones by the way they supported their businesses. And our Consultants had influence over their husbands by the way they talked about and handled their businesses. As Consultants gained more support from their spouses, they built more successful businesses by leveraging their gifts and their strengths. In doing so, they had tremendous influence over those closest to them, including their husbands, partners, parents, kids, and neighbors. Even when these women had a hard time talking about what was important to them or about their dreams for their blossoming businesses, they still got those results. And I believe most of us are influenced by results.

I reminded the Consultants who discounted or completely ignored the power of their influence that there were always other people watching them. They had influence whether they liked it or not, and it was their job (not mine) to steward that influence. The best they could do was to use what they had—to be real, true, and honest in the way they showed up in their work and how they lived their lives.

We also emphasized authenticity and influence in our relationships in the Home Office. If an employee had an idea that was better than anything else we dreamed or strategized or planned, they had the freedom to speak up. Cathy loves to tell the story of Jen, one of our employees who had ideas for how we could make a change in our warehouse process. Jen came to Cathy with an idea and her reasons for why she thought it would make things flow better. Cathy gave Jen the green light to make the necessary changes but asked her to change things back if the flow didn't improve immediately. Of course, it worked. That situation gave the employees who worked around Jen the confidence to speak up and influence our company with their own ideas.

That's what I call a win-win and the power of influence in relationships.

20

CHOOSE

Impact over Image

THE IDEA OF *IMPACT* was so important to us at Thirty-One that one year we designated our annual conference as the "Impact over Image" conference. We had been through a hell of a season in the years leading up to that decision (2015–2019), and we needed a reminder and perhaps a bit of reframing that our understanding of success should include our *impact,* not simply what we had achieved. This came after the big realization I had that our *impact* was different from our *image*. Our image was what people from the outside saw us achieve, and if we were being honest, our image might have been steady, but our impact was slowly slipping.

The original image of Thirty-One began taking shape back when we were working so hard to solidify and define our company values and making corporate decisions based on those values. Then came several years of successful sales numbers, enthusiastic attention from our industry, and glowing magazine articles about our achievements in places like *Forbes*. However, a few challenging circumstances—some I've already mentioned and some I haven't—meant there were days we were maintaining an image that didn't necessarily line up with our impact.

There was an expanding disconnect between the way we were perceived in the public eye and the impact we were having inside our offices and around the world. We were having a growing disruption of our standard two-week order fulfillment timeline. This was due in part to a few operational things we could control, but it was mostly out of our control. We had to make difficult choices regarding impact and image because, as Scott once put it, "Image works from outside in, but your impact works from the inside out. And I think we want to be inside-out kind of people." This meant we had some serious work to do.

Before we get into the details of the difficulties of that season, I must first admit that it was easy for me to get caught up in what others said about us and expected of us. For heaven's sake, I was listed as one of the nation's "Women to Watch." My image had been defined not only by our internal achievements but also by these outside perceptions and expectations. We were known as the "darling of the direct sales industry" and the next direct sales company projected to be a billion-dollar company. With $766 million in sales at the height of our best year in 2013, that seemed like a realistic expectation. Our Consultants and field leaders also felt the pressure of these expectations and the image that came from being a crucial part of Thirty-One. So, when our business took a few difficult turns, I wasn't the only one worrying about maintaining our image. Thankfully, while we all can get distracted with image and expectations, we can ultimately still have an impact. What grounded me in that season of tension between our image and our impact was the motto I made up and often repeated to myself and others: "Every day you choose to be yourself, you make an impact."

As we were growing like crazy in 2010–2013, we achieved crazy things such as being three hundred percent higher in sales than the previous year. We were definitely chasing the ball downhill. But the reality was that growing that fast took a lot of cash and big risks. I already shared some of our internal growing pains, but at the height of our success and celebration, it didn't look like our growth was going to slow down anytime soon. We had an image of fast growth from the strong foundation of a relationship-based company culture. So, we just kept adding more incentives, more programs, and more people. Our growth peaked then began to fall in 2014. Not only had our business flattened, but we were down in sales by twenty percent. Ouch! That's when we felt the heavy pressure of all of our excesses—excess inventory, excess people in our Home Office, excess order-fulfillment and shipping times, and excess resources in other areas.

Rather than immediately making the decision to right-size, we added more incentives and more programs to entice our sales field to sell more and sponsor more Consultants. When that didn't seem to work, we were quick to throw out discounts. You know the expression "too much of a good thing"? Well, we definitely had too much of a good thing going on with our sales field, and we were sinking under the weight of it all. Our sales field couldn't handle the "more" we were throwing their way. Things got confusing, even more overwhelming, and ultimately resulted in more decline. I now understand that we were too focused on our image to see what it took to remain a healthy growing company. We eventually right-sized what seemed to be a sinking ship but not without a lot of mistakes and loss.

Although I learned the hard way that I had to make business decisions differently, we were still having a positive impact on the world. Just because we had a decline and were not fulfilling a certain image or meeting others' expectations, we still had thousands and thousands of women using Thirty-One to help their families with such crucial things as budgets. Many Consultants were still growing and developing personally because of their experience with us.

Our corporate values of *honesty* and *transparency* were important during those difficult times. There was the previously mentioned "Zippergate"—the time we oversold by thousands on a monthly customer special of one-dollar zipper pouches for customers who spent $31 in a single order. Even as we had thousands of zipper pouches on backorder, we kept our online ordering options open for our Consultants and customers. While this was great customer service, it cost our company hundreds of thousands of dollars in extra shipping charges because we were paying to ship the customers' orders and then paying to ship second packages when the zipper pouches arrived at the warehouse. That's how we were living up to our image of providing a great customer experience, even though it ultimately had a negative impact and really hurt the business.

Another time we had to be super honest with our sales field was when we got embarrassingly behind. We simply could not get our new systems up and running to process orders fast enough. We of course nicknamed this fiasco "Shippergate." We gave daily updates on shipping statuses and eventually gave every customer a gift certificate to come back and shop with us once we had things sorted out. But everyone was upset: our customers, sales leaders, and Consultants. To make matters worse, our Home Office team was overworked and really discouraged.

Some of our customers and Consultants lost confidence in us, which resulted in even more business decline as well as people saying unkind things about me and Thirty-One in public. I was so focused on repairing our damaged image and dealing with the hurtful things people said that I began losing confidence in my leadership. I was super distracted by how to react and fix problems and became less attentive to our core values. The biggest problem was declining revenue and profitability. But I was also concerned about our relationships, both inside and outside of Thirty-One. I would lie awake at night wondering if we were still having an impact on families. Of course we were, but I couldn't see that from our bruised image and all that was whirling around me.

I also had to trim down the excess in our Home Office by letting people go. Talk about losing sleep! Relationships were what mattered most in our business, and there I was telling eighty employees they had to go. The spring of 2014 was the first time we had a reduction in our workforce, and I still feel it like it was yesterday. That was not an easy time. But I kept reminding myself that I had to choose impact over image because that was what mattered most.

Ever heard of "imposter syndrome"? On days when I had to make difficult decisions but was being heralded in business magazines and other media, I felt like such a fraud. I never thought I measured up to the image of a multimillion-dollar CEO, but especially not when we were on the decline. A bit of this perspective can be humbling and healthy at times. It's also a huge reason that we are so careful to focus on our impact rather than our image or expectations. As the company began to struggle, I felt like even more people were watching, and there was an even bigger spotlight on me as the CEO and Founder. I had to wake up every day and ask myself: Is what I'm working on having the kind of impact we want to make as a company? If it wasn't, I stopped doing it. But that didn't mean things got easier right away.

At council meetings, leadership talks, and conferences, I was sharing with our leaders how they needed to focus on their impact over their image. But the reality was that I was struggling internally to lead within our values and mission. My speeches to our sales leaders were less inspiration and more about revenue numbers. I was training on more of "what" to do rather than "how" we do it at Thirty-One. Working with Craig, my business coach, was super helpful. But I also had to remind myself what mattered most to me personally—my faith, family, and the impact of Thirty-One. I had to remind myself how I wanted to lead and how I had previously shown up during our peak growth seasons with inspiration. I also had to decide what story I was telling myself about the impact I was having.

I had to do this not only for me but also for my team. Our titles (insert any title—CEO, VP, NED, SED, ED, SD, Director, Manager) came with more pressure and expectations during those stressful seasons. With "Shippergate," our VP of Operations had a lot more expectations to fix it. During "Zippergate," our VP of Sourcing and Inventory carried all the pressure. When we began to lose more leaders than we were promoting in the sales field, some of our upper-level leaders felt the pressure on them. The hardest times for our leaders were when they felt the impact via demotions in their titles or less money in their paychecks. Titles are important to clarify roles and for recognizing success, but sometimes they can create a sense of failure when they change in the wrong direction. It's a difficult part of the nature of direct selling. As business comes and goes, titles change, and if we get too focused on our title (which becomes part of our image), we can lose sight of the drive and passion that made us successful in the first place. As CEO, I had to be honest about our declining numbers, but I still wanted to lead with purpose and keep inspiring others. In that season, I didn't have to personally deal with losing a title like so many of my friends in the Home Office or sales field did. But I felt their burden and wanted to invest myself in leading us all through turning the business around for them and their teams.

One of my favorite books has always been *The Traveler's Gift* by Andy Andrews. I love it because of Andrews' style and the thoughtful questions he asks: *Do you have a decided heart? Is your destination set? Are you committed to redirecting yourself if you happen to get off course?* I have read this book at least six times, and I always have different takeaways. But the quote from Andrews that I kept coming back to was: *Only you can write your story and give yourself time to let your imagination run wild with where you want to go.* It reminded me that my heart was committed to inspire others through Thirty-One and that I was committed to redirecting myself as a leader. This book was what helped me get back on track as I led our company through that challenging season.

Scott says, "We need to learn from our past, but we can't live there." We had to contend with our circumstances of success, then excess, then decline, but we couldn't get stuck there. We had to re-imagine our hopes and dreams for the business, then set a clearly focused plan for how to turn them into an impactful experience while writing the next page of our story and taking the next step on our journey.

Image doesn't always reflect reality, but impact is real. This was true for Thirty-One. What mattered most was how we made someone feel after they encountered us and the impact we made and the influence we had in their lives and for their businesses. We had a giant tapestry hanging outside my office in our New Albany, Ohio, facility with a quote from Maya Angelou: "People will forget what you said. People will forget what you did. But people will never forget how you made them feel." That's impact. Ultimately, when we make an impact on people at Thirty-One, the result creates a lasting image in their hearts and minds.

Julie's stories reflecting impact over image:

> We took the idea of our national "Impact" conference and spread it to smaller gatherings in cities around the United States to connect with local groups of Consultants in their own communities. This was our

best external attempt to maintain our impact with Consultants, even when our image was struggling. We held these smaller gatherings in Chattanooga, Atlanta, Orlando, Columbus, Denver, and Salt Lake City.

We had no idea that our national conference in 2019 would be the last large field gathering (outside of these smaller city gatherings) for three years. There were nearly 9,000 Consultants in attendance at the "Impact over Image" conference, which was our fifteenth national gathering as a company. For those of us who had been to every event, it was easy to get distracted by the work it takes to pull off the event, and we took for granted the joy and excitement of the gathering, simply because we knew we would be back doing it all again the next year . . . or so we thought.

The national gatherings had become an experience that no one wanted to miss. Consultants carpooled in packed vehicles and stayed in hotel rooms with more people than advised just so they could afford to be there in person. One of our goals of the event was that everyone left there with a stronger belief in themselves and Thirty-One. Having a theme in 2019 of "Impact over Image" could be seen as a precursor for the challenging years ahead of us, but in July 2019, no one knew what was heading our way.

PART THREE

Right-Sizing to Stay Afloat

Today, I want you to think about all that you are . . .
instead of all that you aren't.

—UNKNOWN

21

PLAY

Let Your Imagination Run Wild

RUNNING A BUSINESS requires a lot of creativity and imagination. But at the peak of our success and in the middle of our decline, it took every ounce of creativity and imagination we had to keep our playful spirit at Thirty-One. We often talked about how, in a thriving business like ours, we had to be quick on our feet and super flexible. That's why *flexibility* is one of our twelve core values.

Scott, who was trained as a jazz musician, led us to a metaphor of jazz versus classical music to understand a key aspect of the evolution of Thirty-One. He told us both kinds of music require skill, talent, expression, and a solid underlying structure. But a difference between the two is that jazz music is built with room for improvisation and creativity, whereas the structure of classical music (although creative in the hands of the composer) was rigid and didn't often allow for individual creativity. When we were growing so fast and chasing the ball downhill, we needed a solid infrastructure, tight systems, and clear organization, or the whole thing could have fallen apart. But because of the nature of our business—fast growth, an ever-changing sales field, a culture that was constantly changing due to new people coming and going, and the ever-present demands of customers—we had to be willing to improvise over our foundational structure.

Many other businesses could be more structured and rigid, but ours always had to be flexible because there are so many changing variables. When new and unexpected trends in consumer behavior popped up in data trends and sales forecasting or on social media, we had to let our imaginations run wild to adapt to meet the needs of our field and the preferences of our customers.

Experts tell us that our imagination and our metabolism slow down in our thirties. Think about how much we used to dream when we were younger compared to now (speaking for myself here). I can remember how much time Scott and I spent in our twenties, on our honeymoon, dreaming about our future family and life together; we do less dreaming now. It's not that I've quit dreaming. It's just that those dreams aren't as playful or wild as they once were.

This kind of midlife response of slowing down and settling in also happens in the life of a business. I was blessed to have realized so many of my dreams through Thirty-One, and I was content with where God had us, even when things with the business didn't make sense. Knowing that our Consultants were working hard, sometimes with more than one job, taking care of their families with little ones or teenagers, I saw it as part of my purpose to help them get back to dreaming big. I wanted them to let their imaginations run wild. But actions speak louder than words, so I also had to keep finding fresh ways to play and dream in my own life. I had to create space to improvise with my imagination about new dreams for my life, my family, and our business.

How did I keep using my imagination and keep dreaming big as we progressed into a maturing business? Believe it or not, there are practical ways to keep dreaming, playing, and using our imaginations that work, whether we are managing our personal lives or leading a business as big as Thirty-One. From time to time, I had a chance to share these ways with our Consultants. Here are those practical ways to keep dreaming:

- *Make time for an annual "Dream Session" on or around a birthday or wedding or work anniversary.* I've always been a huge fan of such dreamers as Walt Disney. Like those infamous Disney "Blue Sky Sessions" we heard about in books and on tour at the studios, we also conducted annual "Blue Sky Sessions." The magic of these dream sessions is that there are no gray clouds allowed. We understood there were no bad ideas and no perfect ideas, only intentional time to sit down and dream. What helped me was to tap into the playful imagination I had as a child. What were my wild dreams back then? How was I able to make those dreams happen? Research shows that doing this kind of exercise retrains our brains for more of this kind of thinking.
- *Spend non-task-related time with loved ones.* Most of us get caught in the hamster wheel of life and forget to take time to just dream and be creative. I often challenged our Consultants with "Be a dream-maker for your spouse or your loved ones." That also often came up in Scott's HOT class at our conferences. He encouraged husbands to embrace their wives' success, or potential success, in the business as a way to step back and ask themselves what their dreams were. He asked, "How could supporting your wife make more room for you to chase your dreams together?" We've seen so many marriages and family

relationships change through the years as a result of this talk. Many husbands or loved ones started new businesses of their own, found new hobbies, or focused their energy on doing what they really loved beyond just holding down a job.

- *Create a dream board.* On occasion, I did an exercise with our Thirty-One leaders in which we had magazines, printed inspirational words, pens, glue, and poster board. We'd create dream boards, also called vision boards, about what was important to us and where we wanted to invest our time. I had never done a dream board until I attended a Direct Selling World Alliance meeting. We had a great life coach and facilitator, Barbara Pelligrino. She shared her presentation, and we began to open our thoughts about what was important to us. I wasn't quite sold on the idea at the time, but months after the process, I began to understand the value of having a visual of where you want to go and what success might look like for you. My favorite dream board was one I created on an eleven-by-seventeen-inch poster board. I shared it with Scott to make sure I had visually captured the dreams we had been discussing. I kept this board under a tray that sat on a bench at the end of our bed, and I would pull it out every now and then to remind us of our dreams and keep us focused on them. One day Scott pulled out the dream board and pointed out that we had accomplished almost every dream photo on the board. It was definitely a moment of gratitude and celebration. It also encouraged us to realize the impact of putting our dreams out there, even if it meant tapping into our playful spirits and letting our imaginations run wild from time to time. Because this is what it took to stay connected to our dreams.

- *Consider how you can help other peoples' dreams come true.* I never stopped dreaming about what Thirty-One could do for people. As amazing as it was for so many years, I always made room for more. As an Executive Team, we hoped for more people to join us and realize their dreams through our business. I wanted everyone within reach to experience the blessings that this business could bring to their lives.

Our imaginations can't just be wild and all over the place all the time. Using our imaginations to dream actually requires a ton of focus. That's why we encouraged our Consultants to first figure out how they could make the most impact, and then use their imagination there.

Most of our Consultants, as independent sellers, and business owners, would tell you it's easy to get distracted by stuff that may seem important but isn't actually productive. But when our Consultants focused on *everything* they wanted to accomplish, they ended up spinning their wheels because they weren't focused on anything in particular. I believe that when we focus our imagination to create priorities and goals, it can become our GPS. It helps us reach our destination in the most efficient way possible. We can imagine our dream destination, then set our goals around that. And that's what we encouraged and empowered our Consultants to do. We talked about how the way to make our dreams happen was more like the unstructured improvisation of jazz, not like the structured format of classical music. That's why it was always so important to us to leave room for creativity and flexibility along the way, even as we stayed focused on the journey toward those dream goals.

The tough balance for the business in all of this was keeping the structure and systems healthy while still maintaining a playful sense of creativity and imagination. To be honest, we had a hard time with this. There is a certain size of business that requires a lot of corporate structure, and we were at that size on more than one occasion. You cannot maintain a healthy business without that kind of structure.

At the same time, I think we lost some of our imagination along the way. We probably said, "We can't do it that way anymore" too often. We let protocols keep us from thinking outside the box like we once had. The big corporate machine of Thirty-One was much harder to start, stop, and steer than our old speedy ATV (all-terrain vehicle) of a scrappy young business. The stakes were higher, the mountains harder to climb, and the data spoke louder than our deep sense of intuition—always opposing what we knew to be true in our guts. We were good at what we did, but we had lost a little of that reckless, nimble adaptability that defined us through our massive growth years.

At times it seemed the more sophisticated our organization got, the less successful we were. Growth had gone from "just happening" to "difficult and challenging" to "make it happen again." We had all these new shiny tools, very talented teams, a solid organizational structure, and a well-known brand, but the growth was slowing us down under the weight of its challenges, and I started to worry. As our business grew to $700 million-plus, there was nothing to do but get those creative juices flowing again. We needed to be more agile and able to adapt and change to meet the needs of our Consultants in a split second.

We believed so fully in the pursuit of our dreams and tapping into our playful spirits in order to let our imaginations run wild that we titled our national conferences in 2011 "Imagine the Possibilities."

It's still one of my favorite conference themes. We focused on giving ourselves permission to imagine what is possible without fear.

I knew if we were going to make it another ten years, we ALL had to let our imaginations run wild with "what could be" at every level of the organization. But encouraging our teams to be imaginative and brainstorm new ideas was hard when we got into the execution mode. We were implementing so many projects, new product lines, catalogs, programs, and incentives just to stay afloat that most of our meetings became more about short-term goals.

Julie always helped me get our execution plans to our project managers, and she was also the one to help us get out twelve to eighteen months ahead. At one point, Julie and I created a new meeting cadence to drive the different stages of strategic planning while, at the same time, not miss out on using our imaginations.

That cadence went something like this:

1. Our first set of meetings were called the "Plan It" phase (we internally branded this as **PlanIt**). These meetings included top-level leaders from key departments such as Product, Marketing, Sales, Legal, Information Technology, and Operations who would gather for several hours at a time for brainstorming and Blue Sky dreaming. This phase happened eighteen to twenty-four months ahead of time. At this stage, we would recap the last season, look at data about what worked well and what didn't, then brainstorm about what was possible. We tossed around new innovation and "what if" ideas. *What if systems weren't the issue? What if cost wasn't an issue? What if our supplier had unlimited capacity? What if people were unlimited?* Julie brought in case studies from other companies in our industry for us to learn from and get our brains working.

After brainstorming, we would prioritize our ideas to create a plan. This phase was similar to deciding where to go on vacation. *Where do we want to go, and what do we want to do? What's the purpose of this trip: to relax, explore, be romantic, catch our breath, have some fun?* The **PlanIt** phase was the big blue-sky space we needed to let our playful spirits emerge and our imaginations run wild.

2. The next phase of this strategic planning was the "Map It" phase (internally branded as—yep, you guessed it—**MapIt**). Let's say we had a few big ideas that came out of our **PlanIt** phase. This was the time to map it out. It included a set of meetings usually twelve to eighteen months out from any product reveal or event roll-out. One of our first meetings in the phase included a briefing for the projects we had prioritized in the **PlanIt** phase with all of the directors of each department involved in the prior planning session. These briefs included itemized lists of required resources, estimated costs, team members involved, potential lead ideas, and a rough timeline. This was the stage where some projects died and others would grow legs and move forward. Using the trip analogy, this is where we mapped out our itinerary and logistics: how we would get there (plane, boat, or car), the travel directions, and some ideas for what we wanted to do once we arrived.
3. The next phase, known as **DriveIt**, was for the projects that were moved forward. Managerial teams from each department became involved. After input from all of the managers, each project was given to our Project Management Team to "Drive It" forward with a series of

meetings. This was full-on execution, or as we like to say around Thirty-One, it was "all hands on deck."

It should come as no surprise that Julie was a key player in every phase from **PlanIt** to **MapIt** to **DriveIt**. We had all three phases going on at once because we were always working on the next twenty-four months out while driving to go live with current projects. It was like driving a car to the destination with the full itinerary in hand, each hour planned out to maximize the trip, even if the planned time was for rest and relaxation. Without this kind of planning, it was easy for ideas, dreams, and goals to lose their priority and momentum. We needed a strategy to maximize our creativity, and the "PlanIt—MapIt—DriveIt" strategy is what worked for us.

Looking back, just a few years beyond implementing everything, I'm so inspired by the work we did with that new strategy and by the way our Consultants were willing to join us for the ride. Watching them realize their dreams while we realized ours at the corporate level, I realize we made a collective impact on the world *together*. It always amazes me how God gives us dreams and then way over-exceeds those dreams when we let God push us outside our comfort zone. I had a dream for Thirty-One that required a lot of imagination and faith, but what it became between 2003 and now is far beyond anything I ever expected. God definitely exceeded my dreams, even when there were difficult parts.

I'm so grateful for the ways we maintained our playful energy throughout the years, like the time we celebrated our tenth anniversary at our annual conference in Atlanta in 2013. Our theme for that year was "Experience the Celebration," and we had larger-than-life versions of our most popular products so our Consultants could do just that—experience the celebration. Everyone got to climb inside giant-sized purses and totes. Not only did this make for great photo ops, but it made for imaginative fun.

For our fifteenth anniversary in 2018, we did a pink truck tour across the United States. We had a hot pink truck with a hot pink trailer that converted to a pop-up shop. Our team drove across the country stopping in every possible location where there was a substantial number of local Consultants so they could not only shop our products, but introduce their community to Thirty-One in a fresh, playful way. Of course, everyone who visited our hot pink pop-up walked away with fantastic free stuff. This was how we maintained our playful energy amidst the hard climb and decline of corporate sales, especially when we had to right-size our business model to stay afloat.

22

CLIMB

The Mountain

I'VE BEEN ASKED many times when I knew our business was going to be successful, and my answer remained consistent. My goal was to have a profitable business by our fifth year. We worked consistently to reach that goal. Even though it was such a short time, we stayed focused and crossed that line safely in the middle of year five.

Beyond our initial five-year foundation of success, our growth over the next five years felt like pure momentum. We weren't doing anything to specifically grow the business, except just being ourselves and focusing on our purpose to encourage and empower other women. Our insane growth was the result of that ball rolling downhill and us just trying to keep up and execute. But when the momentum stopped for the first time, we had to double-down and focus on a hard climb to get our revenue growing again. The hard climb for revenue started in late 2013, after our pinnacle years in 2012–2013.

After a few years of small "operational" hills to climb (i.e., our sponsor freeze, "Zippergate", and the future "Shippergate"), rebuilding the revenue of Thirty-One was the biggest mountain we had to climb. My family loves to hike, but I had never actually climbed a mountain before then. But, because of my love of learning, I had studied mountain climbing and read about the strategic packing, pacing, and persistence required of climbers. So, this became a helpful metaphor for me when things got hard—when we had to climb the mountain of success with the business. Stay with me for a few minutes with this metaphor.

When we started Thirty-One, we had to "pack light" because we didn't have investors or the spare cash to add too many extras. We were pacing well with slow and steady growth because we had not yet experienced the momentum. It took persistence to stay focused on our (well, my) five-year goal of being a success. Then, fast forward to our ten-year mark with all of that momentum from our massive growth, and we were very heavy on assets, inventory, and resources. Needless to say, at one point, with over $60 million in excess inventory, we were not packing light for our climb back to growth. It was like starting on a challenging hiking trail at the bottom of a mountain with the heaviest backpack load you could imagine.

Pacing ourselves as we climbed up the mountain was not even a consideration because our sales decline was worth more than the cash, we had saved to run the business. We were in the negative and had to get out fast. Our initial reaction was to depend on short-term fixes like product sales to sell off older inventory and drive quick revenue dollars, but we did this far too often. This was only a temporary bandage over a bigger wound. But one thing we still had after our first big climb up to the mountaintop of success was *persistence,* and it would serve us well as we handled the decline. I was not willing to throw in the towel. The livelihoods of our Consultants and employees were far too important to me. So we pressed on with our climb.

Winston Churchill, former prime minister of England, once said, "Mountaintops inspire us, but valleys improve us." I had learned so much as a business owner and leader those first ten years. But now

I was faced with the difficult reality that my lessons were no longer helping the business grow in this new season without momentum. Some years felt flat. We weren't growing, but we also weren't declining. Other years, the terrain felt rougher. But I didn't want to let the shadows between the peaks keep me from moving forward. After all, one of my personal mantras is to just keep putting one foot in front of the other.

I learned that there were two choices after finding myself at the bottom of the mountain and longing to be back at the top. I could either be sad we came down the way we did, or I could turn the new perspective we gained into fuel for the energy we needed to keep positively impacting the lives of others. I think if I had chosen to be sad, I would have crashed and gone into a depression. My way of coping with this tough season was to work hard, stay positive, and be willing to make the tough decisions necessary to keep the business going.

This was difficult for my family, and I had to reprioritize a few things. All of the work required to get to the mountaintop in the first place and then to get through the tough season of decline took a lot of my time away from my family. Not only did I have to be intentional about the decisions we were making with the business, but I also had to be—and *wanted* to be—intentional about my time at home. I was on the road at least one or two times each month while the kids were in middle school and high school. I was probably gone for at least a quarter of the year in any given sales season. I missed breakfasts and dinners with the family, lacrosse games, and cheering at Friday night football games—and believe me, those football games were a big deal in Ohio. I understood these sacrifices were necessary for our business, but I needed extra support and planning to ensure my time at home was well spent.

We had amazing help. Jackie, our nanny, brought organization and peace of mind to our home, especially when things were turbulent with the business. She handled such basics as getting our kids to dentist appointments and ensuring they had lunch money on their school accounts. And her presence, reliable assistance, and closeness to our family enabled us to deal with two other major areas that were life-giving for our family when things with Thirty-One were difficult.

First, having Jackie help us with our day-to-day lives gave us the capacity to make quick transitions from work to family at home in a heartbeat. There were days I would meet the family at the airport on my way home from a business trip so we could fly together to Disney. Jackie would have the kids all packed and ready. Other days, I would be driving like a crazy woman on my five-mile commute from the office back to the house, where my bags would already be packed and waiting in the car, thanks to Jackie, so we could head straight to the mountains for a ski weekend. But the best transitions made possible by Jackie were the simple ones, like coming home to a house in easy order. The clothes were washed, folded, and put away. Dishes were done. All the basics were taken care of. I could effortlessly walk into the house, drop my bag, grab a glass of wine, and sit on our beautiful porch with the kids for a family meeting or just catch up on the day.

Second, Jackie's support empowered us to host people in our home on a last-minute basis. One that was particularly meaningful to us was, for several years while Alyx and Evan were in high school, we hosted weekly Young Life gatherings on Wednesday nights for seventy to eighty kids in our home. This group was how our kids found close friends, a collective sense of belonging, and their own love for Jesus. Jackie provided the magic that enabled us to do this.

We enjoyed connecting around food, themes, and dreams, and Jackie helped us throw the best parties and dinners—kids' birthday parties, graduation parties, sales leader dinners, Executive Team lunches, and departmental breakfasts. In these ways, Jackie also had an incredible impact on our Thirty-One family too. We hosted many dinners with our Thirty-One leaders and held strategic planning meetings that included meals with our Executive Team. The bottom line: We LOVED hosting people in our home, and Jackie was key to making it all happen. I share so much about Jackie's help because we would never have been able to make the hard climb up the many mountains of Thirty-One without her and the many others who supported us in that season.

Julie remembers just how special these moments were in our home, thanks to Jackie's help:

> A special tradition I have fond memories of were the times the Monroe home was opened for an exclusive annual dinner event for our Presidential Advisory Council. Being awarded a spot on this council was a huge accomplishment, but the personal invite to the Monroe's home was a coveted reward. The group of twenty to thirty Consultants who were high earners arrived at the home with a small team of Home Office staff there to greet them. The catered meal was top of the line, and the presentation of the dinner was exceptional. Photos of the entire group were taken and framed for each council member to have as a special memento. Most evenings included special added entertainment, whether it was a magician, dancing, a top-secret early product reveal, or just extra time socializing. Those were special memories in the Monroe home, for sure.

When I think about the mountains in my life, I am not thinking only about the metaphorical mountaintop of success or the hard climb we had to make back up after ten years at Thirty-One. I also think of literal mountains. I have so many fun family memories from the lessons I learned on the slopes. When we moved to Ohio, we had access to a small ski resort nearby, and we decided to learn snowboarding.

Talk about learning something hard when you are in your thirties! I felt like I stayed on the easy green terrain for EVER! Eventually, we decided to head to Colorado and Utah to see the beauty of the mountains and try some longer. WOW! God spoke to me so much during those ski trips. He reminded me how BIG He is and of the massiveness of His calling on my life. I believe this is true for all of us and God's calling on our lives.

One day while snowboarding in Park City, Utah—after almost taking out the kid who walked in front of me as I got off the lift—I made a crucial decision. I realized that I wasn't conquering this mountain the way I wanted on a snowboard, so I tried skiing instead. I had skied only once in college, but I was on some of the best slopes in the country. It didn't take long to pick up skiing, and soon I was moving from the easy green slopes to the blue terrain. I wasn't falling as often as I did while snowboarding, and my kids weren't waiting as long for me to make it back down to the lift. Over the years, I invested a lot of time learning to snowboard and ski. It was important to me because this was something I could do with my kids, who had sacrificed so much for me while I worked hard for my dreams and our family dreams. I wasn't going to give up—not at work and not on the slopes.

Those actual mountains taught me lessons that helped me to face the many metaphorical mountains on my life journey. I learned to be mentally packed and ready to go at a moment's notice to tackle a hard climb. I gained an understanding of the benefits of being nimble and flexible, depending on which technique I was using on the "slopes"—skiing, snowboarding, or dealing with a challenging business situation. I discovered preparation and planning were fun and exciting, but the hard part was practicing—on the mountain and in life. It took discipline. I'm quick to get bored, impatient and even cuss(!) while practicing for a hard climb *up* or a challenging ski *down* any mountain. This was true literally and figuratively for me.

I love extending this mountain-climbing metaphor to the business side of my life. In less than fifteen years, Thirty-One went through almost every up and down imaginable. I wish I could say we did it all gracefully with no wipe-outs or falls. But I can say that every climb we've made has been worth the effort. And every time we got to a higher place on the climb, we had the blessing of a new and different perspective, a wider view of God's glory, and a panoramic vision of what else was possible. This was true even in the midst of our decline.

Scott often reminds our Consultants that as much as we love the view from the top of the mountain, the reality is, *we don't live there.* Most of our lives are spent in the spaces between the peaks. And we had many spaces between our peaks at Thirty-One. For example:

- There was the recruiting and sponsoring freeze, and the time we had to shred excess inventory so it wouldn't end up at TJ Maxx and simultaneously compete with our Consultants for sales.
- There was the time we launched a new "higher-end" brand, Jewell, that ended up being a temporary distraction for all of us, and our now-infamous Windsor Argyle Kit flop, which ended up being the worst print in Thirty-One history. We had to offer an alternative enrollment kit because so many people objected to the print. *Who knew?!*
- There was the catalog season we offered a men's line, without much success. And the massive re-adjustment we had to make with compensation and incentives, much to the pain and frustration of our sales field.

- There was the time we tried a Spirit line for our customers who loved their team sports. The concept was solid-color core products that could be personalized with collegiate logos, but we quickly learned that there was a very high cost to maintaining collegiate licensing for schools all over the country.
- Then we tested a product called Studio Thirty-One. Internally, we called it our "flaps and straps" concept because the product had several core purse styles with interchangeable zip-on flap closures as well as straps that could be swapped out. The concept was great, especially for someone who loved variety, but the appeal didn't hit the mark with our customers.
- And perhaps our greatest valley was the drop from $766 million to $400 million in annual sales over a three-year time period between 2013 and 2016.

We've spent plenty of time in the valleys between the mountaintop experiences. But those valley experiences can never take away the joy and inspiration we gained along the way. I wish getting to the top wasn't so hard, but I love the views when we reach it. The mountaintop experience of impact as well as the life skills and lessons we've all learned together along the way have definitely been worth the climb.

23

RIDE

The Wave

BESIDES GOING TO DISNEY and being on a mountain skiing or snowboarding, our family's other favorite outdoor adventure is being on water. We've spent many summer days boating, paddleboarding, or simply playing in the pool.

When the kids were eight and ten years old, we had an opportunity to take our first trip to Hawaii, where we were introduced to surfing. Surf guides taught us how to get up on the surfboard, but that wasn't the hard part. The most difficult parts are knowing when the right wave is coming toward you and paddling your arms like crazy to catch that wave. Believe me, I paddled like there was a shark about to take a bite out of my bum! This was way more challenging than it sounds because my legs are my strength, NOT my arms. It was exhausting using those weaker muscles, and it required a lot of *practice*. Now I want to look at the momentum of growth and tumultuous decline we experienced using the metaphor of waves.

In the heyday of growth at Thirty-One, there was a seemingly perpetual tidal wave of momentum. Consultants were constantly joining our team, and it felt like the product was selling itself. Even with all of the challenges of growth I mentioned earlier, I'd be lying if I didn't say it was so much fun. I loved seeing dreams take on lives of their own. *Yes,* we were busy beyond belief. And *yes,* on a daily basis, we were making huge changes to how we operated. But those changes were about responding to our growth, not doubling down on the details of what was and wasn't working well. As long as orders were getting to customers and Consultants were making sales, we didn't have time to stop and get all fancy with our systems or evaluate the small details. Because we were climbing the mountain so fast, it honestly felt like it was all working. So why stop? We were too busy keeping up with the business to do anything else.

All anyone from inside the business and those looking in from the outside could say was "Wow!" We had a special thing going at the start of Thirty-One. Our Consultants knew it and felt it, and that's why they were so excited to share our story and our products. And our employees were overall very happy. Even though they were working hard, they did it with so much passion. It was no longer difficult to find good, skilled people to work for us and with us. We had talent coming from other direct sales companies because they wanted to be part of our explosive brand. Our tidal wave of success looked like a lot of fun to them too, and they couldn't wait to work in a place that was both successful and had a great reputation for a healthy organizational culture like Thirty-One.

There was so much energy when we were riding that wave. It was exhilarating. The wave was so strong that it didn't feel like we had to push. Our Consultants were seeing so much success with both selling and recruiting that we just rode the wave of momentum. Of course, as we experienced years of great success, we still worked hard and continued to improve our operations, marketing, training, and communications.

When the business was booming and sales were great, I felt confident to take my focus off Sales and Marketing and learn other areas of the business. I found that when the Sales and Marketing team was ahead of their sales goals and beating their plans, then the Operations and Technology teams were stressed. But if I shifted my focus off of Sales and Marketing, including Product Development and Design, we began to lose our momentum as a company. Taking focus off of whatever drives the business is dangerous no matter what size business you have. Our eventual sales decline and our reactions to those downward trends felt similar to falling off a surfboard. It happened fast, hard, and it spun me around underwater. Not a great feeling to have.

The downturn of business at Thirty-One required what felt like swimming back out to sea, looking for another wave, and then paddling my arms like crazy to get back up on the board when I found one. In business terms, our downturn required me to gather my Executive Team, develop robust real-time and short-term strategies, and make decisions based on actual financials rather than staying focused on the overly abundant care and compensation of our Consultants.

We did a lot of hard work to re-align all departments, get input from our Presidential Advisory Council, and build a management and communications strategy to set us up for a new wave. Up to this point, launching and communicating new strategies was less than ideal because we were *reacting* to the business rather than *responding* in focused and intentional ways according to our annual plan. New strategies didn't always go smoothly. There were times we launched a plan and then had to backtrack, unwind the plan we had just rolled out and start over again. All for the sake of staying afloat.

As we encountered our own difficult waters in those turbulent years of 2013–2016, I found a YouTube video by Les McKeown, an author and business growth advisor, talking about how to create what he calls "Predictable Success," which is also the name of his best-selling book. He discusses several stages of success, including one he calls the "whitewater" stage. This resonated so deeply with me. McKeown helped me categorize the challenging season we were going through as a business and gave me a label for the solution to my leadership problem.

I wanted the people around me to help us bring the material in McKeown's book to life. I shared the white-water analogy with our Home Office team, Consultants in the sales field, and even with peers in our industry. I hoped that in sharing it with the people around me, someone would have additional advice on how to get out of this phase and move on to predictable success. Inside Thirty-One, we were always working on our internal strategy, and as a result of what I was learning, we developed the theme of "rowing all together." This was the sticky metaphor we needed to move through the white-water rapids we were experiencing. I knew we all had to metaphorically "stick our oars in the water" and "row together."

We went so far with these themes in April 2016 as to buy small wooden oars for each team to present their departmental goals. They wrote their goals in sharpie markers on the oars and presented them in front of the other managers and executives. Then we hung the oars on the walls of our Home Office in each department as a visual reminder of their focus for the year. We gave every employee our one-page Thirty-One annual plan with our theme of rowing together to promote the plan and gain traction while staying focused and unified. This season of unifying around a clear and common theme enabled us to stabilize the business and plan for future growth. It was a memorable experience for all who worked in our Home Office at the time.

I was so proud of how everyone rallied together in this season and helped us move the business forward.

Even though our Consultant numbers started to decrease just a bit after our decline, we were still 70,000 strong in 2017. This group of encouraged and empowered microentrepreneurs and dreamers were known to use their focus doing good and giving back. And in 2018, we sold eighteen million units, a solid number for us. It was a reminder that anything is possible in this business.

The second hardest period we had to endure was the span between 2018–2021 when our business was dropping in revenue and the number of Consultants. It seemed as though the waves were coming fast and hard. But choosing the right waves to catch and successfully riding them required flexibility, practice, and getting back on the board time and time again. We made tough decisions to right-size our budget, re-size our teams, and adjust other resources to support the revenue each following year. We had to pull our resources back to almost half of what we previously were spending and investing in. It might have been easier to do all of that at once, but we chose to pull back each year as was necessary. This allowed us to target the specific areas where we had room or needed to pull back.

Again, this required flexibility from all our teams who were working so hard to help us drive the business. But it also caused waves of staff reductions. Ouch! It was so hard any time we had to make the decision to reduce the size of departments and teams, because we had built more than a company and more than a bag. We had built a *family*. We gave everyone who had to leave Thirty-One as much love and support as possible. Some people understood, and others really struggled—understandably so.

As people left the Home Office team, we had to clarify roles and move seats again to keep our community and collaboration strong.

People felt disconnected across a sea of empty cubicles, so we made moves to reconnect them. Many of those who remained in their jobs had to work through "survivors' guilt" and missing their work friends. I was so proud of how gracious, loyal, and committed to their work they remained through those hard times. We always had truly good people.

The end of an era at Thirty-One for some meant the beginning of a new season or career for others. Our remaining Home Office team members who took on new responsibilities as a result of the downsizing got promotions and the chance to develop new skills. We encouraged everyone to keep asking questions as they changed roles. "That's how you learn. Never stop learning because that's how you grow," I heard myself saying over and over again. Our employees were growing personally and professionally, and it was like fresh wind in their sails. I could see everyone learning to ride their own waves in addition to the big wave we were riding together as a company. I was reading more books and asking more questions to figure out how to lead best in that season—a season unlike any I'd ever experienced before. I knew if we were going to be good at finding waves and safely riding them back to shore, we all had to continue to learn and hone our skills.

Whether we were riding a great wave or being knocked off during the white-water phase, Thirty-One was not only our purpose and passion, for most of us, it was our ministry, one of the big things God called us to do with our lives. We had changed the industry from the stigma of pushy salespeople to difference-makers during our time building Thirty-One. Whether it was in our first big rise, our frustrating fall, or our steady rise again, everyone who interacted with us knew that, as a company, we were *more than just a bag*. And climbing back to a successful year of sales gave us the ability to pause and make margin as we considered the future of Thirty-One.

24

PAUSE

Make Margin

MARGIN IS SPACE YOU BUILD into your life to live intentionally and make time for what is most important to you. It comes from setting priorities and boundaries. From the beginning of Thirty-One, Scott and I were always aware of the risk we took of working too much and too hard, and as a result, not giving our family enough time and energy. It has been a tough balancing act throughout our history together.

We took the kids on a Disney vacation a couple months after the business started in 2003, and I still remember the tension I felt for working beside the pool while Scott and the kids played. When Scott was a pastor serving in local church ministry, we saw so many pastors and lay leaders give their best energy and most of their time to the church, often at the expense of their own family relationships. We were determined not to let that happen and committed to creating margin for each other and our kids. We prioritized vacations and other intentional time for just the family, even in the middle of busy seasons. We did our best to create special family time whenever and wherever we could.

Alyx was an early teen when she announced one day that she hated "family time." She didn't hate the time, just the words. So one morning over breakfast, we renamed it "sausage time," which of course got an eye roll out of her. Whatever we called it, we found the best times together were when we got away from home on the weekends. I didn't grow up in a suburban neighborhood, and in Ohio, I missed hills, acres of land, and lakes. So, we purchased a farmhouse in nearby Mount Vernon, Ohio, on 128 acres with a couple of rolling hills, a rare find in central Ohio. It was the perfect place for "sausage time"—weekend getaways to walk, ride bicycles, work on puzzles, and play "sardines" (imagine reverse hide-and-seek but in complete darkness).

We all cherish our "sausage time," so we fight for it, plan for it, and fiercely protect it. It's the least we can do for the tremendous sacrifices our kids made due to our never-ending engagement in Thirty-One. They've always been supportive and forgiving. We can't say for sure, but Scott and I believe that being intentional with creating family margin made a huge difference, and it's the reason we're still so tight today.

We often invited to the farm our Chattanooga friends who moved to Ohio, and sometimes the kids' friends come along. And, as the kids got older and had more weekend plans of their own, we began to use the farm to hold Thirty-One retreats, creating a time to collaborate with our sales field leaders. Eventually, this expanded into our leaders hosting their teams there too. We offered special activities for these retreats, including archery, movies, and karaoke, but one of our favorites was clay shooting. When I personally hosted a retreat, I'd ask, "What is holding you back from achieving your goals?" We'd write down three or four things on the "clays" and literally blow them up with a shotgun. The farm became a place not only to rest and pause from day-to-day pressures, but it was also where we could leave what we didn't want to take with us.

For Julie, pausing and making margin with her family meant moving back home to Tennessee. After having her third baby in 2012, she decided it was time to put her family first—something she felt she hadn't done in a long time. By the time baby Jozie was eighteen months old, Julie and Jason sold their home in Ohio and moved to Knoxville. During that transition, Julie took a step back from the business to be present with her family, exhale, and gather her thoughts. After eleven years of building the business with me, she needed to catch her breath from one wild ride after another. Cathy and I, as well as the rest of the Executive Team, supported Julie's decision as the right thing for her to do. But, of course, we missed her like crazy!

Everyone has their own way to create space for themselves. Here's what I've learned about making margin over the years.

- If I didn't intentionally set aside time in our family calendar, we didn't have any. The saying "The speed of the leader is the speed of the team" was true at Thirty-One and in my family. Scott and I lead in different ways in our home, but we decided that, as the CEO, I would be the one to make margin for myself and the family.
- Getting good sleep was essential for me in every season of leadership. When my head hit that pillow at night, I was usually out within five minutes. But I had to make sure I was consistent with bedtime or it would prove disruptive to my body and my mind.
- I learned from other people. Pastor and best-selling author Andy Stanley uses the example of a page in a book. He encouraged his audience to imagine how stressful it would

> be to read a page in their favorite book if there were no white space on the page—just words crammed from edge to edge. It would be unreadable. This analogy spoke volumes to me. So much of my creativity, dreaming, free thought, and even rest happened for me in the "white space" of life. And with all of the competing noise in my world, a day crammed to the edges made me full of stress, anxiety, fear, and worry. I learned that white space was not only where my dreams were born, it was also where they were mapped out and turned into action.

Margin is where I gathered my strength for the momentum of our business and our lives. But I had a lot of challenges making room for margin. A typical day would be filled with scheduled meetings and hallway meetings on the way to other scheduled meetings. It was overwhelming and exhausting at times, although I found energy in our ever growing and changing pace. That rhythm came naturally for me, perhaps more so than it did for other people. But I was aware of how risky it was to operate without margin for extended periods of time. Without it in our culture at Thirty-One, we rushed things out before they were ready and pushed our Home Office teams past their limits. This was sometimes our knee-jerk reaction, but it wasn't worth it. It would always prove difficult on me, our internal team, our Consultants, and the company as a whole.

In the middle of a messy season in 2014, I had sixteen direct reports. We had removed the C-level titles and everyone below that rolled up to me as the President and Founder. For those individuals, it was good for them to have a direct line to the Founder, but for me, it was just too much. My meeting schedule was out of control, and it exhausted me like no other season. I simply couldn't be my best self for the company. As a result, I made the conscious decision to hire a

President who could focus on Operations while I stepped in to help run Sales and spend more time with the Product team. Regardless of whether or not this helped the business, it was better for me. That season, I learned that *ALL of us need margin*. Books and pages need a margin of white space, life needs margin, and you and I need margin.

The simplest way I've found is to withstand the impulse to check my phone while I'm kept waiting. Most of us can't abide inactivity without grabbing our phones from our pockets or bags to check for new messages, posts, or stories. I'm no expert, but there are plenty of studies that show how much the digital life has impacted us for better and for worse. And filling every quiet space of our lives with our face in our phones is just too much. For all the good that goes along with being connected, constant connection has a negative impact. You are the only one responsible for creating margin in your life, your marriage, and your family. The best version of ourselves is when our margins are open and free.

Now, there are *ways* to make margin and *seasons* to make margin. One of my favorite ways as a family is to have a family meeting where we get to dream, imagine, recharge, and rest *together*. And the holidays were a *margin-must* for us. My parents still lived in Tennessee, and for several years after moving to Ohio we tried to go back for most of the major holidays: Easter, Fourth of July, Thanksgiving, and Christmas. But Scott and I struggled with finding our own immediate family time with the business and my schedule, in addition to frequent trips to visit our extended family. Often these holidays were when the kids were out of school, and we needed to spend those days off together. Our top family priority is to each other and our kids. Our extended families are super important as well, but we had to prioritize. Eventually, I had the conversation with both of my parents that we were no longer coming back to Tennessee for holidays. You might think that was selfish of us, but we believed it was important to give ourselves permission to do what was best for us and the kids at the time. Talking to our parents about changes to our holiday traditions was hard, but it gave us what we needed to pause and make margin when we needed it the most. Of course, we still made time for our parents and siblings, and in recent years have found meaningful ways to connect with them outside of our family time together.

Making margin in every way possible was the greatest gift we gave ourselves when we needed it most, finding the space we needed to reflect on opportunities and challenges.

25

REFLECT

Find Your Inner Coach

IN 2016, thirteen years after starting Thirty-One, I hired Craig, my business coach. I've already talked about how impactful this was in my life and for my leadership, but I want to explain why I didn't do it sooner. For so long, I had trusted my *gut,* which I lovingly refer to as my "inner coach." She is a good one too. But when I started doubting myself during the downturn, I realized I needed help from someone outside the business to find my way back to listening to my inner coach.

During our big tidal wave of momentum in those first ten years, I leaned into my gut and almost always believed in my ability to make the right choices. When business began to decline, I started to second-guess myself and rely more on data and hard numbers. Of course, those are good sources, but I trusted them in lieu of trusting myself. I had to find my way back to the center—*my* center. It seems weird to say it, but I needed an external coach to help me reconnect with the inner me.

Not everyone trusts or even acknowledges their own inner coach. Some people simply don't have confidence, often because of wounding messages or messy life experiences from the past. Tuning into that inner voice can also be difficult with so much noise and outside influence around us. But my guess is, from time to time, we all experience gut feelings of what we know to be true deep inside.

In my early days of leadership, trusting my gut meant embracing my bossy childhood self. Besides personally following my inner guidance, I also gave a ton of direction to others. I was often quick to give advice without being asked, mostly because we were moving fast and so much of the business fell naturally to me. Part of it may have been because I could see some team members didn't believe in their own skills, but most of it was to control an outcome and how fast we were moving. I wanted to see to it that we prioritized growth and efficiency over security. Thankfully, most of the people around me trusted my inner coach. If they considered me overbearing or too controlling (although I'm sure they felt this way at times), we wouldn't have gotten as far as fast as we did. My control and advisory style of leadership was sustainable for many years until our departments and teams grew.

I could no longer attend all of the meetings, make each decision, or provide every bit of direction. I remained in touch with my inner coach for myself, but it was no longer possible for me to dictate those gut feelings to everyone else. I learned from several areas of my life, including coach Craig, how to stop giving advice and start asking great questions. I've always been curious by nature, and from watching others, I came to value the art and skill of asking questions and truly listening to the answers. I have to say that I still struggle with this, but learning to be curious, ask more questions, and listen carefully were all critical to leading a company of our size and fulfilling my desire to be a servant leader.

Becoming a servant-leader was one of my greatest challenges during our season of decline. Serving my team also meant listening to their inner coaches and gathering the data they needed to lead and make decisions with their own teams. The coaching I got from Craig showed me how to be a better leader and coach to my teams as opposed to being their commander. I had a real desire to see them grow and trust them to make balanced, well-thought-out decisions.

Touching base with my direct reports was definitely easier when the business was doing well. But when it began to decline and we were reacting to daily challenges, my controlling leadership style moved back out front. My reactions were to grab the reins when I felt uneasy about where we were heading as a business, and I think this is true for most of us. We default to what comes natural to us and what makes us more comfortable when too much pressure is applied. That's why I hired Craig. With his help, I was finding my way back to me and my inner coach.

It's important to note that, while I learned to trust my gut early on, I didn't always have confidence in my inner coach. That was built over time and then rebuilt as I worked with Craig. I knew our business so well in those first ten-plus years that I was able to make quick decisions and create wins for our team. Each win built my confidence to try new things. Over time, as I realized some people around me needed gentle coaching to trust and pay attention to their own inner coaches, we made it a point to publicly celebrate the wins of our Home Office teammates. We wanted to help them build the confidence of their inner coaches too. Sharing new and successful ideas was always encouraged at Thirty-One because we had a very entrepreneurial culture. If something didn't work, no one was fired over it. We discussed what we learned as a team and how we could approach the idea or situation differently next time. Having this approach helped us all be better coaches—for ourselves and our teams.

Looking back now, we probably could have avoided some of our declining sales had we not only built the confidence of our team members, but also tracked more data and paid attention to changing trends. Hindsight is always 20/20, but there were definitely early indicators of decline had we read our data differently. More insight going up to our decline in late 2013 into 2014 could have helped our internal teams and Consultants with prioritizing their projects and product sales.

When we made the transition to relying more on data to forecast product, style, and shopping trends and built more sophisticated systems, we put into place a Business Intelligence team. Being more data-driven required us to not only "mine the direct sales data" and even build data warehouses, but it also required us to bring in people who could interpret insights from the data. Hence the new team. I'm also the kind of nerd who loves data, because it tells a story. It tells an even better story when you can look at it over a long period of time.

For more consistency in our data, we held monthly business review meetings where each department shared their updates, including the data that supported their projects and goals. At times it felt redundant to share data every month the way we were doing, and honestly some departments probably created their reports just to check them off their list. It took time to truly figure out and embrace how to best gather and use data and then turn that knowledge into good insights. Tracking data balanced with trusting my inner coach became important to me as we found our way forward after the decline. One without the other didn't always get us where I thought we needed to go. But blending the two was an important part of how I found my footing as a leader again.

It's important for me to call out specific insights from the data we mined as I reflect on the early days of my inner coach. I didn't have a ton of data in those days, but I was close enough to the business that I could trust my gut to gather insights from the soft and hard data. Soft data came from anecdotal stories of the Consultants and holding monthly sales field meetings about what was working and not working with our products. Our Customer Service team was also invaluable at helping us gather soft data, as they handled complaints, returns, and compliments.

The hard data came from running reports and tracking the sales commissions we were paying our Consultants. The bigger the company got and the more distance I had from that kind of data, the more difficult it was to listen to my inner coach on behalf of the entire company. It was no longer enough to use my own thoughts and ideas to make major decisions. I had to find balance again with an outside perspective from my coach, so I could help my team develop their own inner coaches. Doing so was vital in giving the business better chances of more success.

I'd be remiss if I didn't mention how important my faith was to the journey of reflecting and finding my inner coach again. There is no doubt that my belief in God and the calling I sensed God placed on my life to start the business was what made all of the success and impact of Thirty-One possible. Psalm 100:3 says, "It is He who made us, and we are His" (NIV). Because of my confidence in God as my creator, I believe we can and should make the choice to believe in ourselves. We can do so because we can believe in who He made us to be. Believing in God, believing what God says about us, and believing in ourselves is a choice we get to make. We get to choose whether or not to focus on the positive decisions we've made, then try to replicate those decisions as we grow and move forward.

Not every decision we make is right. It's important to recognize the right ones, knowing we can be confident in them. When I made major decisions regarding our business, as I still do today, I made sure to include prayer and reflection, data and reports, and the stories and opinions from voices I trusted, including my own. The more decisions I made with confidence, both in the beginning from my basement, through our remarkable growth, and later as we climbed out of our decline, the better I got at making them and the more confident I was in my leadership and decision-making again. The greatest confidence booster I had was to find my inner coach and experience my faith at work.

This season of reflection made me realize I had outgrown the image of an entrepreneur who had it all under control. I had now grown into a seasoned leader who had experienced the high-highs and the low-lows of business leadership and who was now constantly trying to stay balanced between the control of data, the wisdom of my team, and my own deep sense of intuition. Too much of either—data or trusting solely on my own gut—took me back to the extremes.

Sadly, too many of us have never learned or have forgotten how to listen to our inner coach. But we can learn—or *re*learn—to trust ourselves and put faith into practice. There's always something of value to be found, even when we need outside help to get there. Finding our way back to ourselves is always worth celebrating. It's what helps us not only grow up, but also show up for ourselves and for the people and places that matter the most.

26

GROW

Show Up & Grow Up

ONE EVENING during our National Conference in 2016, I brought all of our National Executive Directors (NEDs) into my suite at the Nationwide Arena in Columbus. We served wine and appetizers, and everyone gathered, sitting on every available surface with many left standing around the perimeter of the room. We announced that we were taking them all to China to meet our Atrium partners and the amazing people who made our products—those products they were all so proud to sell. It was an exciting and emotional moment for all.

As we rebuilt confidence in our business and began to concentrate on growth again, we landed on a strategy that included strengthening relationships and a heavy focus on innovation. A trip to China for our NEDs fit perfectly in that strategy. We wanted to spend quality time with them as well as allow them to see the relationships we had with our manufacturing partners to build confidence in how our product was made and in who was making it.

When we left for Jiangsu, China, most of our NEDs brought a guest—a spouse, mother, sister, or best friend. We took them all to visit the factories and the local Atrium sourcing office, and they all got to spend time with the Thirty-One executives who came along.

The factory workers at all of our partner facilities literally rolled out the red carpet for us and gave us unbelievable experiences that wildly exceeded our expectations. We had tours of the factories, met the workers, and witnessed huge piles of our products going through sewing production. We watched our fabrics being made and saw all the steps involved in making our signature product called "Benjamin's wallet." Our time with the factory owners and their teams was priceless.

I vividly remember one of the factory owners, a woman named Amy Lee, sharing about the opportunities she had been given within her family business because of their partnership with Thirty-One. She also served in the local government representing her community because of the reputation her family had earned. She was such an inspiration to our NEDs. Seeing a woman in that kind of leadership position in a place that we didn't fully understand coming from the West touched the hearts of our Consultants and their guests.

We were also able to visit one of the local schools and meet the children of the factory workers. We donated an air conditioner to the school, and the kids welcomed us by painting, dancing, and singing for us. It was a beautiful partnership between our amazing company and the many wonderful families who worked in factories to support us across the world. Jenny Hillenburg, our very first Consultant and one of our NEDs, shared that she was so moved by the idea of someone halfway around the world waking up to begin working on her business while she was falling asleep in America.

It was overwhelming for everyone on the trip to realize the number of families who were impacted by their partnership with Thirty-One. A trip like this was an enormous expense at a time when we didn't have a lot of extra cash to spare, but it was part of our strategy that we would inspire our leaders to continue to invest in their businesses. As a result, it was also our hope that we would continue to climb back toward unprecedented growth. We often refer to that season as the time we had to "grow up and show up"—for ourselves, for each other, and for Thirty-One.

Also during this time, we invited all our new leaders to the Home Office for a two-day event we called Leadership University. These new leaders were given a tour of the office and warehouse operations, and it was their chance to rub shoulders with and be trained *in person* by some of the top leaders in our sales field. I made it a point to attend almost every Leadership University (LU) so I could meet each new leader and take a photo with them so we could put a face with a name. It was important to me to share about my confidence in them and their goals. Many of our leaders say that LU was the experience that helped them "grow up" as leaders and got them started on their leadership journey. LU strengthened relationships, which was an essential part of our company culture and now a strategic growth goal.

For our fifteenth anniversary in 2018, we decided to show up for our top leaders and celebrate them with our biggest incentive trip to date. We went to HAWAII! A total of 772 leaders earned their way to a fully paid, all-inclusive trip plus a guest to Maui. This trip came at a time where we were still struggling with growing the business. The good news was we were no longer in decline, but we weren't growing yet either. We still needed more new Consultants joining Thirty-One. The trip was over the top and such an incredible time. Our first goal was to make everyone feel celebrated with their hard-earned reward (check!), but we also hoped the trip would help drive new sponsors and increase product sales. But the big splash of Maui just wasn't enough to regain that momentum. It was huge for some of our teams, and it strengthened relationships, but it didn't grow the top line revenue numbers.

Another way we showed up with our leaders as we celebrated our fifteenth anniversary was by driving our hot pink truck and trailer on tour across the United States. We already mentioned the tour earlier, but what I didn't tell you was where the tour ended that year: *at our 2018 National Conference*. It was fun to see our leaders out on the road as they introduced our brand and products to their actual neighborhood community from our pop-up shop in the trailer. Even better was greeting everyone at the conference arena in Ohio as we were coming off tour. Even our driver became a huge Thirty-One supporter. I wish I could say that the tour worked wonders for our numbers or led to an uptick in fresh ideas and new Consultants. It didn't. But it did strengthen our relationships with the people who already loved our brand.

We now realize we probably should have hired an expert on something so big and outside of our wheelhouse as rebuilding sales and revenue after a massive decline. We didn't, but we did have a good return on investment when it came to relationship strategies developed during our decline, especially with Leadership University.

Another way we really started to show up more fully in the business was with our innovation. It received a lot of our attention and focus on our rebuilding years. As customers began to buy fewer of our products, we thought it could be because they had one too many of our large utility or thermal totes. Our Consultants were struggling to tap into new customers in their communities and kept going back to their same customers. The Consultants were very vocal with the Home Office about how they wanted new products to add to what they were offering their customers, *our* customers.

With these requests in mind, there were several ways our product team worked to bring innovative ideas to create new products. A group of Home Office employees met weekly regarding new personalization options, new product ideas, and new prints they found. They brought those ideas to the brainstorming table, and I personally worked on acquiring other brands or bringing in existing product lines that would be fast to implement into our system. We started offering jewelry, home decor with personalized pillows, wood products, baskets, and other home storage solutions. We sold a lot of products with these new categories, but it wasn't significant enough to create the momentum we needed to build our revenue back up to where it once was. This was the point in our company's story where I started to "bang my head against the wall" trying to figure out how to motivate, move, and inspire our now 40,000 Consultants to get excited about the business again.

In the spring of 2018, we were significantly impacted by tariffs placed on imported goods. Unfortunately, this meant we would have to make difficult decisions. We kept looking at expenses, knowing our top two expense lines were our *cost of products* and *commissions* paid to our Consultants. We had to consider those. Product costs were not going down so we couldn't reduce them. We were forced to consider changing our compensation plan for how our Consultants received their commission. This was something we desperately tried to avoid. In fact, we did everything we could for years to take care of our Consultants at all costs, even when that meant we ate extra costs as a company. But in 2018 we were still in a difficult financial position and needed to drive more sustainable behaviors with our Consultants. We had to show up and consider the hard things in order to keep growing up as individuals and as a company.

On one hand, being overly generous with compensation plans translated into a cash problem. Between 2003 and 2018, we hadn't reserved a lot of cash in the business because we were committed to new technology and generous compensation rates and incentives for our Consultants. But those generous plans and incentives weren't always scalable with the rate of our growth. So, after our massive decline, then a plateau, then another slight dip, we had to right-size our expenses. At first, we were still committed to buffering our Consultants from the impact of our decline by delivering the incentives and the compensation they were used to. But our generosity turned into a sense of entitlement for some, and it became our catch-22. I had to re-invest some of our personal money back into the business, which was not the ideal plan, but it was critical to staying afloat.

Those days of fluctuating sales in 2018–2019 were challenging, but we did our best to keep our business going. Along the way, I made many difficult choices that I never thought I would have to make. Nothing makes us grow up faster than facing difficult decisions. I was growing up as a leader and fighting hard for everything we could use to turn the business back around. I was showing up more than ever for work and to invest in the relationship side of Thirty-One. And that's what helped us clarify our next steps and determine what mattered most.

27

CLARIFY

Determine What Matters Most

CLARIFYING WHAT MATTERED MOST in 2018–2019 started with a decision we had to make in 2017. In the midst of trying to figure out how to stabilize the business after our decline–growth–plateau–slight decline again, we learned that our landlord—L-Brands at Easton Commons in Columbus—was not interested in renewing our lease. While I was struggling to adjust our expenses, invest in our sales field, keep up with new product innovation, and maintain my sanity as a leader, I now had a new project whether I wanted it or not: *find a new space.* And the options were a bit more complicated than it sounds.

We first had to ask ourselves a few essential questions, such as: Which would be the best decision and investment—to keep our Home Office and warehouse distribution center all under one roof, or separate these entities into two separate spaces? We brought in experts to help us first map out all of the options for our distribution warehouse and then figure out what to do with our Home Office departments. We considered moving the whole operation an hour south of Columbus. But not everyone who worked for us in Columbus would be able to drive an additional hour to and from work, and the population in that particular area could not support the number of jobs required in our personalization departments we needed to move with our distribution center. And we didn't believe there was another viable warehouse distribution solution in Columbus. Not even in Ohio.

We researched metro areas large enough to support the number of jobs we needed in Arizona, Nevada, Texas, and Tennessee. When we mapped out the shipping destinations for most of our packages, it quickly eliminated our options in Arizona and Nevada. Tennessee, particularly Nashville, would be a stretch for finding a building appropriately sized for the number of employees we needed, plus the UPS/FedEx shipping zones didn't align well for us from there.

Dallas, Texas, kept popping to the top of the list on every front. So, I made a trip there with our VP of Operations and a few real estate experts. We found several options, but one building stood out more to me than the others because of what the surrounding community could provide. It seemed like the best fit for our needs and our company culture, and I could picture us as a vital partner in that community. Time was ticking, and we had only a short timeframe to make our decision and begin the move. So, Flower Mound, Texas, northwest of Dallas, would be the location for our warehouse operations and distribution center.

A few of our operations had to change in the move. First, we needed an efficient picking and shipping system. For this, we had to eliminate some jobs we had in place in Ohio and shift to high-tech equipment, which would create long-term savings and efficiency that helped to offset the additional money required for rent in Texas. Replacing people with machinery is never an easy decision, but moving facilities made this more doable because there would simply be fewer roles to hire for at our new distribution center.

We relied on experts to help us get the systems, equipment, and new processes up and running so we could make the transition as seamless as possible for our customers. We had a huge celebration when everything was in place in Texas and the first order was shipped out of the new facility. The original plan was to have seven months of overlap between the new facility in Texas and our existing one in Ohio. Considering our struggle to rebuild our business, we knew this was going to be an expensive transition, but it seemed like the best situation for the long run.

We had NO IDEA what was really ahead of us.

Over the next few months, we sent more monogramming machines and printers to increase shipping from Texas. We were up to a shipping rate of thirty percent of our packages from Texas when our VP of Operations suggested we could speed up our transition if we shipped everything from one place for our 2019 summer outlet sale and our fall catalog launch. We went back to the data, looking at the numbers and projected sales, and forecasted output from our new facility. It all appeared to work on paper, so we made the decision as an Executive Team to move up our date to be running the operational side of the business one hundred percent from Texas by that summer.

The orders kept coming in, and we were super proud and excited about the possibilities of our new warehouse. The automation was impressive, and it felt like we had figured out how to be a technologically advanced and sophisticated operation. We had come so far from our days of physically printing out orders and laying the order papers on boxes as they moved manually through multiple places and many hands around our warehouses in Tennessee and Ohio. The time and energy we poured into new innovation seemed to be paying off . . . until we began to see bottlenecks in the automated lines. There were traffic jams in the new warehouse, and this was not a good sign.

We had orders piling up in monogramming, which spilled over into shipping. To reduce the backlog, we hired more monogrammers and trained them as fast as we could. But because they were all new to the job, they simply were not producing near the same volume of units our experienced monogrammers in Ohio were able to produce. I spent a ton of time flying back and forth between Ohio and Texas to add an extra set of eyes on how we were moving orders through the warehouse. It was helpful for me to assess the situation and communicate updates to our Consultants. Shipping orders started backing up. Days turned into weeks, it was unacceptable how far behind we were on orders with thousands of frustrated Consultants and disappointed customers. It was a full-on "Shippergate" situation.

This was not our first shipping delay by any means, but this time it was big, and it was not getting better fast enough. We launched our new fall catalog without some of our new products in the hands of our Consultants, which meant it was hard for our Consultants to book new parties when they didn't know how/if/when shipping was going to get better. We were maxed out in Texas and in over our heads. We spent millions of dollars to find solutions and fix our lines. At that point, we were already a bit fragile after our first major sales decline, and we were no longer bringing in new Consultants and booking new home parties at the same rate we once did. We were *struggling*.

Our sales leaders were amazing during this time. Most of them were patient, and they realized this too would pass. They trusted our team to figure it out. When you are in sales, you depend on the company to deliver what you are selling, but it is your reputation at stake with your customers and team. Our Consultants and leaders were being asked to keep selling without knowing when products would ship. We got past this season, but as a result of the delay, our sales declined, our customers and our Consultants lost confidence in us, and we hit a cash crisis. This was definitely one of our top five major challenges at Thirty-One.

When I pulled back to clarify the situation in my head and determine our next steps, the only thing I could think about was saving our Thirty-One legacy. I started this business with Julie by my side because I had a dream of creating an opportunity for all women. The first eight years between 2003–2011 flew by, thanks to pent-up product demand and hyper-sales growth. But we didn't realize that pace wasn't sustainable. When we hit our first decline in 2015, it required us to stabilize, get focused on the business, and lean into our relationships. For three straight years, between 2015–2018, we were close to being stabilized. But slow distribution in a new warehouse cost us millions of dollars we didn't have to spend, as well as the confidence of our closest community, our sales field.

I wanted our Consultants to understand that we made all of these decisions with them in mind, even the ones that led to our decline. But I knew I had to frame it in a way they would understand. In 2019 at our National Conference, I told the story of my wedding band. It reminded me of where Scott and I came from and those early years together in Soddy Daisy, Tennessee. Both of us came from working-class families who loved us and taught us an amazing work ethic. During the Texas transition, as I was feeling like our business was broken, my wedding band actually broke from wearing thin. I kept wearing it and struggled with the idea of getting a new ring. I wanted and needed more time to think about it. For most of my life, I had been the kind of person who always had a quick reaction to life's problems. If my band had broken in a different season, I probably would have been quick to get a new one. It was the same with business decisions: If something was broken, I wanted to fix it fast so we could all move on. But at this time, I wanted more time to thoughtfully respond to declining situations—including my broken ring.

When Scott and I celebrated our twenty-fifth wedding anniversary in 2018, we took a cruise along the Italian coast, leaving from Rome. We traveled in May, right before "Shippergate." I needed the vacation and our marriage needed time for us to be together. After twenty-five years, I was still happily married to the guy who had first asked me out on a date when I was just 15. Before the cruise, as Scott and I were walking around Rome, an incredibly romantic city, we saw several jewelry stores. Scott asked if I wanted to go ring shopping to replace my broken band. I said "Sure, we can look." We went into Tiffany's, Harry Winston, and a few other stores. This Tennessee girl was trying to take it all in without knocking something over. I had never been offered champagne, a velvet chair to sit in, and served chocolate truffles in a dome-glass serving dish anywhere before, especially not in a store. I thought, "Am I in a movie? I didn't even get dressed up!" We looked at several rings, but I didn't want anything flashy or elaborate.

My original wedding ring was a square princess-cut diamond, and I kept asking for that shape in these stores. We were in Harry Winston and they showed me several rings. One caught my eye, although the diamond wasn't my preferred square princess-cut. At a closer look, I realized this ring looked square because the prongs were shaped into an H on one side of the band and a W on the other side. The salesperson told us it stood for "husband" and "wife." Are you even kidding me?! This ring was personalized with initials, just like the personalization we sold on so many bags as our signature mark at Thirty-One. I really liked that ring, but I couldn't decide on the spot. We left the store to think about the purchase overnight. Plus, I wanted to make sure I wasn't just dreaming that I was in some kind of romantic movie.

The more I thought about it, the idea of a new ring—*that* particular ring—symbolized where we wanted to go versus where we had already been. The thought of this ring and wearing it with the W facing me each day would be a reminder of my commitment to Scott and my desire to be a great wife. We didn't know where the business was going during those turbulent times, but we were solid in our marriage and knew where we were going as a team. So, we bought the Harry Winston H and W ring.

I told this story to an arena full of Consultants because I wanted them to hear that it is okay to consider something new—a new ring or a new way of operating—and rethink something they've been doing for a long time. While my old ring was still beautiful, the band was broken, and I simply couldn't wear it anymore. I needed something new if I wanted to wear a wedding band. I will always treasure my original ring, but Scott was so proud to buy me that new one . . . and in Rome! This was significant in Thirty-One because I was considering how to maintain our existing relational culture and legacy, while being proud to bring innovation, new perspective, and fresh ideas.

Over the next year or so, in 2019, I was doing a lot of soul-searching. I created a job description for myself for the first time. I spent time clarifying what mattered most to me: my faith, family and Thirty-One. I had been working so hard at doing things to fix the business, and I had in some ways lost vision of the person and leader I sensed God made me to be. Best-selling author and teacher Joyce Meyer says, "You have to separate the 'do' from the 'who.'" That reminder translated into our business too. We were so desperate to make things happen at Thirty-One that we had been "doing" ourselves deeper and deeper into what felt like a scary situation. We had to get our focus back on what mattered most for Thirty-One and put that focus back on the "who."

There were surely things that were out of our control, things we couldn't turn around no matter how hard we tried. But as Scott says, "The opportunity was still there for the taking." In the fifteen plus years since we started the business, buying trends had changed, there were new entrepreneurial ideas, new regulations. We had to be open to anything and everything as we carried out our vision and created new opportunities in the business to encourage and empower more women.

Clarifying our sales field meant we were focused on growing back to 70,000 Consultants strong again, but this time with a fresh and modern approach. We wanted to *expand* in some of our new markets, namely the West Coast. We wanted to *sponsor* new Consultants and *retain* existing Consultants who represented the diversity of our nation—women who came from all different backgrounds, ethnicities, and experiences. We wanted to *develop* strong leaders again, *increase* our sales, and *evolve* our sales model to keep up with the current times.

Parties were the best way to scale our business, and we realized that parties didn't have to happen only in person. They could also happen online, and Facebook was perfect for online parties. We already had over five million customers who loved our products, but we knew there were more who would love them too, if only they knew about Thirty-One. We created a team to focus on building online programs and platforms to help our Consultants grow their businesses while we were still trying to clean up our operations mess in Texas. We offered free shipping as a fun surprise on our million-dollar sales days. And we still found ways to *celebrate, encourage,* and *reward.*

In the meantime, we were still searching for the magic button to turn our business around. Our Home Office team moved into a new office building in Columbus within a few months after we moved warehouse operations to Dallas. And now we were working our tails off to mend the gap, provide solutions, and find new revenue streams.

28

CHANGE

Be It, Do It

DID ANYBODY ELSE grow up with the old adage that women are more likely than men to stop and ask for directions when they are lost? According to this stereotype, men, due to pride or stubbornness, will keep driving even if they don't know where they are going. As to whether or not this is a proven fact, I'm not so sure. I do know that I'm the kind of gal who is quick to stop and ask questions. I'm a planner, and the minute that my plan isn't working, you better believe I am asking for directions.

Over the years, I've asked for directions from my Executive Team and Board members, not to mention other amazing leaders in our industry. But at some point, the directions everyone gave me just weren't getting us to where we need to go, which was back on track to grow our business and regain momentum with our revenue. We needed more direction.

By 2019, I had invested most of our family's "rainy day" savings back into the business, and there was not much left to give. Some of our Consultants were asking tough questions about adjustments in their compensation, which meant they had to tighten their budgets too. Many of them had to reduce their house payments and right-size other family expenses. Some of our Executive Team transitioned to different companies while we battled to figure out how to get Thirty-One back on track financially. Honestly, a few on our team were scared, and I couldn't blame them. As a business, we were all just trying to stay afloat, in big and small ways.

By fall of 2019, I was desperately asking myself and those around me why we were struggling to turn our business around and make a profit again. I wasn't getting solid answers. We were running out of capacity with our vendors and the bank. I was running low with my own energy and faith, which was hard for me because my faith has always been my superpower. I believed in our team, our Consultants, and their sales teams. I also believed in our culture and what we built as a company. And, quite honestly, I had always believed in me. I had more knowledge and wisdom in 2019 than when we first started. We had stabilized the business before. *So, why was this time different?* I couldn't get things turned around using the resources, tools, and business acumen that seemed to work so well in the past. So I had to make hard decisions if we were to move forward. I may never know why I wasn't being given answers for how to turn this business around, but I'm so glad I kept seeking.

In Spring of 2020, I quietly reached out to Kanbrick, a business builder company, to invest in Thirty-One. This was the best and only way I knew how to keep us afloat. Kanbrick wasn't the first company I had researched, but I had a sense it was the one to help us climb out of our financial situation. I was very clear in what I wanted, which was a team that would be our "partner" and invest their time, energy, and hard work into turning the business around. I wanted a long-term investment from someone who had experience with a successful business turnaround. I was pretty sure I found the one, but it took a few months of conversation and negotiations before we could talk about this idea with the rest of our team beyond the Executive Team and, eventually, our Consultants. So, life and business went on like normal . . . as normal as it could be at the start of 2020.

That January, Scott, and I became sick, and it seemed like more than just a standard cold, sinus infection, or flu. We hardly ever got sick, so it was already unusual. The urgent care doctor in Park City, Utah, where we had recently purchased a home, said it was a strange new virus that was going around, not the flu, and most people coming into the clinic had it. So we took our vitamins and cold medicine and showed up at the Thirty-One Leadership Summit that month anyway. Scott may have felt horrible, but he played his heart out for the worship and dance party we held at the summit. The following month, there was talk about a new virus all over the news called Sars-Cov2, or the Coronavirus, later known as COVID-19. By March, the country was shut down.

We had already been planning some difficult but necessary changes in the ways we were doing business to get us through this season. Here's how Julie remembers that time right before the big global shutdown:

> At the beginning of 2020, Cindy shared the business struggles with the strategic team that I was a part of. We worked hand in hand to create a change in management communication that would go out to the Consultants. It all revolved around the date of March 1, 2020.
>
> In January and February, as we worked through every Consultant-facing aspect of the business that we would announce changes for, we didn't know the March COVID-19 shutdown was looming. Cindy shared that we were entering a revenue turnaround effort and had to pull back on expenses dramatically to right-size the business.
>
> The customer special discount was too deep, so we had to reduce it. The Insider (party host) discounts were too deep, so we had to adjust them. The sales incentives to earn free products would have to go away for a while. And the elaborate incentive trips the Consultants

> had been working to earn for the past decade were put on hold. The commissions-override structure for our leaders was too costly to sustain, so there were huge adjustments made there too. This heavy news we rolled out was just part of the bigger picture of rebuilding the business to sustainability.
>
> Our Consultants knew that when a message came directly from Cindy, it was news they needed to hear. She had a tone that got their attention—we call it her mama voice. Magically, she could encourage and reprimand all in one sentence. But she did it with a tone that clearly showed how much she cares. Our Consultants heard and responded to the seriousness of the news. They continued to be supportive and do what it took to keep moving forward. Even in the hardest times, I felt blessed to have a leader like Cindy, who put her heart and soul into communicating through a season of change, no matter what.

Our Consultants had already endured the less-than-perfect move of our distribution center to Texas, massive delays in shipping, and a few other not-so-positive changes to help with the budget. Now, we were telling them they couldn't have home parties either, due to COVID-19. Like everyone else in the world, we thought the global shutdown would be just a couple of weeks, maybe a month at most, before we would be hosting parties again. But weeks turned into months. If we were going to survive as a company, we had to "pivot"—the 2020 word of the year for every company and entrepreneur.

Some Consultants were already doing parties online and didn't feel much of a negative impact on their business or see the big deal about going all online. They were happy that the rest of the world was home too and saw it as an opportunity to start using social media and Zoom calls even more. Meanwhile, other Consultants were struggling to regroup with their businesses. So many of them had spent the last ten to fifteen years building their business through relationships talking around a kitchen table, catching up on porch swings, or sitting in the living rooms of their friends' homes. To ask them to connect, share the opportunity, tell their jokes, and create laughter and community through a computer or a phone (for those who didn't have a computer) was absolutely absurd. They decided to pause and wait until the pandemic was over to kick up their businesses. Little did we all know just how long that wait would be.

While COVID shut down the world and moved us all to online video meetings, we increased the number of times we connected with our Consultants, field leaders, and internal team. With so much uncertainty, it seemed necessary to meet weekly with our employees to give them updates on projects and new CDC guidelines. I also set up weekly meetings with our National Executive Directors to help facilitate how they were showing up as leaders and navigating this uncertainty. We continued our weekly Zoom meetings with our leaders to keep communications consistent and strong.

While the pandemic was good for many companies in our industry that sold household products, kitchen products, or immunity/health supplements, it had the opposite effect on us. It was hard to sell our totes and bags when no one was leaving their house, traveling, going to the ball field, or taking lunches to the office. Our products were not the solutions that families needed when they had no place to go. So, we got creative with our household organizing products and quickly saw low inventory on our organizing cubes, which meant they were selling well. We even used some of our fun fabrics to make masks but were a little late to that trend.

Despite some of these challenges, our Consultants were amazing. To help sustain their businesses, they continued to show up with fresh online party ideas like bingo night or kitchen classroom ideas. Some of our Consultants even offered fundraisers to donate products to frontline workers, including nurses and teachers.

We knew that with all the uncertainty and instability we couldn't cancel our annual conference. Our Consultants needed encouragement from us, and we needed them too! So, we put on our first virtual conference. When I say virtual, it was *all* virtual! Our favorite house band traveled to our home and played in our living room while social distancing, all so they could be part of the conference that year. It was a challenge to maintain the fun interactions and our inspiring calls to action, but we did our best. I prerecorded recognition awards with various groups, and we even prerecorded an interview with Jenna Bush Hager, co-host of *Today with Hoda & Jenna,* from our living room. Each one of our guest speakers sent us personalized messages to play for the Consultants. It wasn't ideal. It didn't include face-to-face smiles and heart-to-heart hugs, but we all showed up and shared our deep commitment to the mission of our company.

I continued talking with Kanbrick as our potential investment partner, as we went back and forth in a few rounds of negotiations. At that point, the only other people involved in the conversation were Scott, our CFO, and our attorneys. It was the most difficult thing I had ever done up to that point, and I couldn't even talk about it. I would wake up at night—which I never do—get out of bed and go up to my office. This was a particularly sensitive decision for me because Thirty-One was such a part of me, and the idea of giving it up to someone else was hard. I would play out scenes in my head of how I had failed and hadn't been a great CEO. Then I would imagine scenes of the company doubling in size with a partner-investor where everyone had the opportunity to be a part of a growing brand once again.

I tried to put my emotions in a box and do what was best for our employees, sales leaders, and Consultants. And what was best for everyone was to bring in a investment partner. After hours and hours of discussions, we had a deal on the table with Kanbrick. You may have seen deals made on *Shark Tank*, but this deal was not one of those giant windfalls. And yet, it was a chance to rescue our business and partner with amazing executives who had experience turning around direct sales companies. It was a chance for fresh eyes on product innovation, sales field initiatives, and our brand. I chose to put my trust and confidence in Kanbrick, a long-term investment partnership company founded by Tracy Britt Cool and Brian Humphrey.

Kanbrick was a new investment company, but both Tracy and Brian had previously teamed up to turn around Pampered Chef, so I knew their hard work and honest reputation preceded their brand. Pampered Chef was acquired in 2002 by Warren Buffett and Berkshire Hathaway. Tracy worked with Buffett in several of his companies and assumed leadership at Pampered Chef under his care. She became the CEO, and Brian was hired as the CFO. Together, they learned the party-plan business model inside and out as they reversed the decline of Pampered Chef back to profitable growth for the company alongside their sales field.

Both Brian and Tracy were up front with me that the Pampered Chef turnaround did not happen overnight. They were confident they could help Thirty-One, and they were also willing to share some of their learning and struggles. We decided that while they would assume roles as active partners and investors at Thirty-One, we would hire a new CEO. I would remain active as the Founder and most recent CEO of the company. It was a hard pill to swallow at first, but this was our best option. And I was actually excited and energized about the partnership with Kanbrick.

As an entrepreneur, I love change. I love taking risks and thinking about new possibilities. I had the trust and respect of our Home Office and our Consultants as I led us through change in the past.

But this time was different. This big change was coming at them after a couple of rough years and in the middle of a worldwide pandemic. Everything was unknown, and everyone was being asked (or told) to pivot. Not to mention that the media was talking about people lying and undermining authority in every direction regarding the pandemic and the political climate in the United States. This was by far the hardest season I have ever experienced as a leader. But bringing in an investor-partner was a sacrifice I was willing to make to preserve the Thirty-One dream for our current and future Consultants.

We were making a lot of changes to our Home Office team, and as Kanbrick was onboarding with Thirty-One, they were learning about us, and we were learning about them. I was in support of many of the changes they were making right out of the gate because I knew we needed fresh eyes and fresh thinking around the business. We brought in an interim CEO to help us with this first year and started looking for a long-term CEO. It took us more than a year to find one, but it was important to find someone who had experience with turning a business around and a solid fit with our merging culture. Camelle Kent joined us as our new Thirty-One CEO in 2021.

With the new leadership and pace of change at Thirty-One, along with the unknown in the world due to the pandemic, it was simply too much for some of our employees and Consultants. Several of them left for opportunities at other direct sales companies or new careers. I get it. I read plenty of business articles and case studies about the number of career changes during 2020 to know we were NOT the only ones experiencing this kind of rapid change and transition.

Looking back, I am so thankful we were able to bring in investors to navigate the uncertainty from COVID-19 and build a strong strategy for growth. I'm grateful Tracy and Brian were willing to come alongside our brand and take the reins to help lead Thirty-One onto a bigger and brighter future. This was the hardest thing I went through since starting the business, but I know I made the best decision for the Thirty-One family.

For me, this transition was like empty-nesting and sending my youngest child off to college (which also happened in 2020) or into their own career and family. I have always told myself, "I can do hard things." I kept reminding myself of Philippians 4:13, which says "I can do all things through Him that gives me strength."(NIV). I needed God's strength, and He definitely carried us through this season of transition. We not only had to think about change, but we also had to *be it* and *do it*. And now, we're better for it and ready to see where it leads!

Here is how Kanbrick Co-Founders, Brian Humphrey and Tracy Cool Britt remember the time:

> When Cindy called us in spring of 2020, the world was in a challenging spot – COVID was bearing down and the uncertainty that was ahead perplexed many. But, at Kanbrick, we were immediately intrigued by Thirty-One Gifts.
>
> We had followed Cindy and Scott's story and how they had built Thirty-One focused on their principles and delivering for Consultants and customers. We admired their approach to building the business, and we saw potential in helping re-build the brand and the business.
>
> When we started Kanbrick, we didn't set out to buy any direct sales business. In fact, we had planned to focus in other areas, but after a conversation with Cindy, we sensed the potential and were intrigued. After a few more conversations, we were even more excited by the opportunity to partner with Cindy to build Thirty-One together.
>
> We saw the strength of the brand, the power of the field organization, and the excitement the products brought to customers. We also saw the challenges the business was facing internally and due to the rapidly changing external environment.
>
> Despite the challenges, we were confident in the strength of the core of Thirty-One and we were excited by what we could achieve

together and with our coworkers and Consultants. We think in decades not quarters and believe great companies are built by people not in spreadsheets. At Thirty-One, we started by building upon the organization's strong foundation while also investing to build an enduring purpose driven organization.

29

SHARE

Lessons Learned

THE NO. 1 LESSON I LEARNED while growing Thirty-One is that the best way for me to lead is by inspiring others. The idea that we are *More Than a Bag* is real, authentic, and the foundation of Thirty-One's success. My biggest ah-ha is that God can use the most unlikely or least qualified to be the vessel for impact. Not only have I experienced and seen that impact on individuals throughout Thirty-One, but I have also seen the impact our business has had on marriages, families, adoptions, communities, other companies, and the direct sales industry as a whole.

Leading this company has been one of my most rewarding roles in life. I will always treasure being a wife and mother above my career but having the opportunity to empower and encourage women to be their own business owners brings me so much joy. It's been an incredible journey to move others to do things they never would have considered or to overcome their fear because of something I said. I have learned to pay attention to what drives me, and step into more than the ten percent of my potential that Mary Kay talked about. I am proud that I did not lean into what the world expected from me or what my grade point average said about me. I am proud that I was willing to lead past the statistic that eighty percent of businesses fail in their first five years. I am overwhelmed that more than 100,000 women said YES over and over again to the Thirty-One opportunity. And I am humbled that employees chose to work at Thirty-One. So many people across the years chose to stay loyal and connected to our company, even beyond their time with us. This still amazes me today.

I often think back to the struggles we had as a business that ended up making us stronger as a company—struggles that made me a stronger leader. I think about mistakes I made that taught me to use better decision-making filters. I think about the times I leaned too hard toward the data and what other people thought. And I think about the times I could have asked more questions, been more patient, and not relied only on myself so much. Thinking about all of this is what makes me want to encourage and empower others to keep going. If everything had been perfect, I may not have been able to relate to CEOs whose companies had experienced the financial and operational struggles we were experiencing. But if everything had been doom and gloom at Thirty-One, we never would have impacted the tens of thousands of people we did.

We could have capsized our boat during the whitewater season or fallen off the surfboard with every giant tidal wave of momentum, but we didn't. We stayed the course and stayed afloat. We also could have reached one billion dollars in revenue had we made different decisions, but that's not how our story goes. And honestly, the could-haves, should-haves, and would-haves are all behind me now and behind all of us at Thirty-One.

My mantra today is the same as it was ten years ago, that I will keep putting one foot in front of the other and keep moving forward. I will continue to use my gifts and talents to inspire and love others beyond my role as CEO.

And because I get asked a lot about our journey, here are a few parting lessons I've learned along the way, some new and a couple favorites from previous chapters ::

- Be careful not to push others beyond where they are comfortable or beyond where they may want to go. Seeing someone else's potential does not mean they see it or are willing to chase after everything required to reach it.
- Ask more questions and give less advice. Asking questions allows other people to find their own inner coach and learn the tools of digging below the surface to find answers.
- Plan for the unexpected and be ready for whatever the outcome may be, good or bad. This is important not only for your budget and resources, but also for you. I learned that when I had considered the worst-case scenario, I was better prepared to lead.
- Cash is more important than revenue. We survived our initial dips in revenue because we had a great CFO who protected our cash. Even when we were overly generous and gave compensation and rewards above what our budget allowed, our CFO kept us afloat. Finding a balance in this is so hard, especially when at the end of the day, it all belongs to God. But the point is to be wise, not reckless with generosity.
- Establish a strong company culture with hard work at the grassroots level. This has been something that many people could relate to and were inspired by. They loved our servant leadership and the way we actually cared about other people.

- Engage with others to hear their stories. I kept going and dug deep because I listened to the stories from our sales field of how they were being impacted. As a leader, I want the feedback that fuels my passion.
- Be willing to stop and ask for directions.
- Communicate transparently with your team and your audience, especially during seasons of change. Maintaining trust with your team is more difficult during seasons of uncertainty. I learned to lean into communicating and collaborating during these times.
- Know your niche. Know who your customers are and why they want to buy from you.

I firmly believe that learning should always be part of life. I never want to stop discovering new things and figuring out what it takes to move forward. There are literally thousands of lessons we have all learned through Thirty-One so far, and there will be many more ahead. I just want to stay open to listening and recognizing when there are lessons hidden in everyday moments. I hope that I'm always willing and able to share what I've learned for those who come behind me. And I know I speak for the rest of the Founding Mothers when I say we want to leave a legacy that's packed with inspiration and knowledge.

30

LIVE

Leave a Legacy

WHENEVER I THINK ABOUT leaving a legacy, the first things that come to mind are our twelve core values. When our success started to settle and wane a bit, it became important to lean back hard into our mission and our brand—and by this, I mean our purpose and our story. As time marched on, we realized the need to define more clearly the culture upon which we originally built the company, regardless of how our numbers fluctuated. We gave ourselves some guardrails by adding behaviors to our twelve values.

But before we get to those behaviors, I'd like to just say we were fully aware of the experts who said companies should stick to three to five values. While that may have worked at most places, our intimate family culture demanded more definition. And we couldn't go any smaller than our set of twelve values and behaviors that reflected how we worked together. These twelve values were how we moved forward toward success. So, here's how we defined our values with behaviors when it mattered most:

Purposeful: *Think and act intentionally.*

Passionate: *Despite obstacles you may face, act with heart and desire.*

Authentic: *Be you. Be real.*

Thankful: *Appreciate all the blessings you have been given each day.*

Courageous: *Stand for what's right and what you believe in, even if you are standing alone.*

Flexible: *Be accepting of change and willing to embrace it at a moment's notice.*

Respectful: *Consider others first and treat them as you would like to be treated.*

Hard-working: *Do whatever it takes to see a task through until it is finished and finished right.*

Generous: *Display a servant's heart.*

Curious: *Seek new opportunities and new ways to expand your mind.*

Fun-loving: *Enjoy your life and focus on the positive.*

Accountable: *Take ownership of your actions and be open-minded and willing to listen.*

To us, these twelve values were a *set*. You couldn't focus on one without the others. If "fun-loving" were the only value practiced by one of our employees or Consultants, they likely never got their work done. That individual also had to be both accountable *and* purposeful in their work. We recognized that, just like personality traits, everyone had a value or two they are more naturally inclined to display. But our goal was for everyone to find different ways to live out each one of our values at various times. Most people don't know that we had a thirteenth value: Trustworthy. We decided, however, that it was already one hundred percent an expectation of every person we brought into the company culture at Thirty-One. Plus, twelve values nicely matched the twelve months of the year, so each month, we highlighted a value and celebrated the employees who championed that particular value.

We applied these values to time spent with our Consultants too. We once had our Consultants do the following exercise to emphasize our values:

- Look at the list of values and rate yourself from 1–10 on each one.
- Take the two or three lowest scores and try to find ways to Intentionally encompass those values into how you work, show up, and treat others over the next week.
- Now, ask yourself what life might look like if you could move those weaker values up the scale this week. How would that impact you and those around you?

To us (Cindy, Scott, Julie, Cathy, our families, and our team), these values exemplified the Thirty-One way, and it was all about being a servant leader and making a positive impact in the world with the people God allowed us to influence. Although we created these for the Thirty-One company and family, we believe these values are applicable to anyone who wants to live a purposeful life of impact on others. While some companies used values and emotional language to manipulate their sales teams, we were far more concerned with imparting good values and inspiring a healthy organizational culture rather than improving sales performance to make the company or anyone else "rich."

Our mission, vision, and values have served to keep us focused on staying true to what we believed was a calling from God: to encourage and empower women in their business, in their homes, and in their communities, through Thirty-One. Our twelve values and their defining behaviors were our way of keeping the main *thing*, the *main* thing: a right-sized perspective of success.

As we mark twenty years in the business in 2023, the guiding mission at Thirty-One is to *simplify the day, celebrate the moment*. And that's what we plan to do, moving on. Thirty-One will continue to be *More Than a Bag* for many women, their families, and their communities.

We have found so much joy in this business over the years and will continue to find joy through our new products, fun prints, our helpful solutions for everyday living, and the amazing business opportunity we offer for micro-entrepreneurs throughout Thirty-One. We are still committed to supporting our Consultants at every moment of their business venture with us. That's why, when a new Consultant joins our team, we work hard to help them find their own flexibility and financial stability in today's busy world. We love that our products are used in a way that brings personal joy when walking into work, showing up for kids' sporting games, or organizing at home. We have built this business on celebrating, encouraging, and rewarding each other on our journey together. And we will continue to do so in the years to come!

By now, I hope that anyone who knows me and everyone who has read this book understands that my desire in life is to inspire others to lean into and live out as much of their potential as possible. I want women to feel confident, take risks, and know they are capable of doing amazing things. Thirty-One has been a wonderful blessing for me and my family. It has exceeded my wildest dreams (it also gave me a few gray hairs!). While I have learned more from this experience than anything else in life, now you know that it hasn't all been easy. But I wouldn't change it for the world.

Turning the page for me as Founder includes having more time to focus on my beautiful relationships—old and new—at Thirty-One and being open to all that God has in front of me. I can't imagine a life without Thirty-One. But I do know that there are more women who have yet to consider the idea that there is more out there for them: more dreams, more joy, more struggles, more fruit, more, more, more. Just like them, I need to remain open to MORE. And if you've made it this far with me in this book, I hope that you are open to MORE too. I hope that you find yourself in a place of being proud of what you have accomplished and thankful for the learnings and mistakes. I pray that you find your own value, confidence, and entrepreneurial spirit from reading about my journey.

While I shared these stories from my perspective, I could have never experienced all that I did without the amazing people who have been on this journey with me. There aren't enough pages to name everyone who has been with me along the way, but I'm so very grateful for the Consultants, the Founding Mothers, the employees, the Thirty-One sisterhood, and the friends who have stood with me the longest and still support me today. This crew will always have a special place in my heart. I will always have a life board of people who are my go-to trusted advisors in life.

As Founder of Thirty-One, I will continue to show up and share my passion for what we have built. I will continue to carry our amazing products, share my confidence in where we are going, listen to our Consultants' stories, and, of course, hug as many people as possible.

So, dear reader and fellow Consultant, thank you for being on this journey with me. I am so blessed that God has put so many people on this path to achieve greatness. I couldn't be prouder of where we are! And we still have so much to do and so much to build together.

We get the chance to leave a legacy with the way we live our lives, the way we take risks, the way we dream. And at Thirty-One we get to leave a legacy by encouraging and empowering women. I wouldn't have it any other way.

31

TURN

The Page

OKAY, DEAR FRIENDS, here's what I want you to hear directly from me: Each and every one of us has many "blank" pages of life ahead of us. Pages yet to be written as we live our lives. I pray that you seek those pages with ALL of YOU as you move through your beautiful and messy life. May you find yourself curious with your mind, loving with your heart, and active with your body.

I know from my own experience that leading a fast-paced life and living with blank pages sometimes means I show up with only part of me. I like to be busy and sitting still is frustrating and depressing. It causes my body to be agitated. So, many times during transitional seasons of turning the page, I would find myself looking to be busy, rather than living in the balance of loving the transition with my heart, learning and being curious with my mind. But my hope and prayer is that you have the courage to show up with ALL of YOU.

Being around a lot of people is both energizing and exhausting for me. Most days, I find it quite draining. If I have to be around a lot of people for extended periods of time, I can get cranky or short with my attitude. Take for instance, If we're at a dinner with a full crowd, it would be easy for me to hide behind my glass of wine to smooth my uncomfortableness with being around too many people for too long. Don't get me wrong, if I've been at dinner with any of you, I want you to know I love and appreciate each of you. But I also like you best when we can connect one-on-one or in a group setting of eight or fewer people. I crave quality time, and quality time with people I love is even better. It does give me energy. Quality time with others allows me to be curious about topics or share love through chatting about your season of life or simply being together.

I believe that love has a special job in our lives. Without love, I think we struggle to find our passion for being curious.

While turning the page of a new season, new week, new month, or new year holds excitement for me, for Scott, it comes with sadness that a season is ending. Like so many, he has a tendency to get stuck in the previous season before turning the page. I tend to turn the page too quickly or rush ahead of others or God. Sound familiar to some of you? When I am quick to turn the page, I find myself waiting. *Waiting for what?* Many times, I don't know. I am just ready to be somewhere new.

So, what do I do while I am waiting? Well, . . . let me go through the unhealthy list first: I find myself mindlessly eating or drinking a little too much wine, watching shows I don't normally watch, shopping online, or the worst, simply whining and complaining. I'm not often a whiner, but if you catch me whining, then I am probably waiting for the next big thing to happen, yet not sure what I am waiting on. Once I get through that stage of self-indulgence and focusing on me, I can usually get myself out of that stage because I am tired of focusing on me. Can anybody else relate? I then move into being curious about what's next on that blank page, which typically includes reaching out to my life board for inspiration and their fabulous questions. I go back to listening to great books or podcasts that inspire me. And I get out my calendar, which marks that I am taking my next steps forward on the blank page in front of me.

For now, that blank page is the life I get to live as the Founder and past-CEO of Thirty-One, and whatever comes next as we move forward with the help and guidance of Kanbrick. I cannot wait to see what these next few chapters hold.

I hope the next time you are in a season of transition and turning the page that you can be aware of what is holding you back, the thing that can get out of balance, and most of all what moves you forward. I pray that you are willing to give yourself permission to *dream*, permission to *take risks*, and permission to *let go* of a few things holding you back.

I have so much confidence that at Thirty-One we will continue to live out our mission of encouraging and empowering women. I imagine a future of so many women (and men) who have yet to experience the Thirty-One sisterhood. I can imagine the fun, new experiences, and new friendships that will be anchored by our Thirty-One Gives efforts. And I believe in Thirty-One because I believe in you. I believe in all of the women who want to be entrepreneurial. I believe in everyone who wants to be successful by supporting one another, and people who want to be a part of a great brand doing good.

What a blessing it has been to write this book and remember every single person who has been on this journey with Thirty-One. I am overwhelmed with gratitude! In fact, we are ALL overwhelmed with gratitude!

So, here's my closing "benediction" for you:

Blessings on each one of you.
Blessings on every employee, every Consultant and sales leader.
Blessings to every vendor who helped us get to twenty years!

And blessings on those who are working with Thirty-One
to live out our amazing brand and values today.

I pray that we continue to be open and inclusive as we bring in all those who are meant to be woven into our Thirty-One fabric. This experience truly has been *More Than a Bag*.

ACKNOWLEDGMENTS

Our Dream Team

Blessed to have Julie and Cathy on the journey with me.
To my loving family, Scott, Evan & Alyx. SeaC forever.
A special thank you to those who took a huge leap of faith and moved from Tennessee to Ohio with us to grow Thirty-One:
Our three other Founding Mothers—Laura, Erin and Kim—as well as Brandon, Brian, Dale, Dean, Deb, Erich, Ham, Jen L., Jen M., Karen, Kristen, Rodney, Sherra, Tim and Tommy.

We are celebrating and honoring our Leaders who have been with us on our journey for 10+ years, as of Dec 2021.
Their names are listed below.

AIMEE NEWTON • ALEXA WILLIAMS • ALISON MCNAMARA • ALISON KING • ALYSON HALL
AMANDA HENSON • AMANDA MCCLURE • AMANDA PILGER • AMANDA THOMPSON
AMANDA ELMORE • AMI BEERY • AMY MURRAY • AMY SORENSEN • AMY WEISE • AMY MERCIK
AMY MEYER • AMY PINKSTON • AMY LITCHFIELD • AMY HANSEN • ANDREA HINES • ANGELA DELONG
ANGELA ELLIS • ANGELA OURTH • ANGELA DURHAM • ANGIE KERR • ANGIE MCLAMB
ANGIE BAILEY • ANN STARE • APRIL TRAVIS • APRIL MCQUADE • APRIL NAYLOR • APRIL KACZMAREK
ARLETTE DAVIS • ASH FEHNEL • ASHLEE ANDERSON • ASHLEY HALEY • ASHLEY EDWARDS
ASHLEY GUYETTE • BARB MAURAIS • BARBARA PROIA • BECCA NEMECEK • BECKY HERNANDEZ
BECKY PETERSON • BECKY BYRD • BECKY SHULTZ • BETH REED • BETH WARNER • BETH ROTH
BETH BRAMLETT • BOBBI TRISKO • BONNIE SCHULZ • BRANDIE TRENT • BRENDA WELKER
BRITTANY ERSPAMER • BROOKE MONSEWICZ • CALLY SLAUSON • CANDICE KENNEDY • CARLA ECK
CARRIE MARTIN • CARRIE HAMLEY • CARRIE BEQUETTE • CATHERINE POLITTE • CATHERINE HAUSCHILD
CATHERINE SZESZULSKI • CATHERINE MADDEN • CATHY RORKE • CATHY O'NEILL • CHELSEA WILES
CHERIE RABERN • CHRISTINE GAMBILL • CINDY MARBURGER • CINDY MARTIN • CINDY PETER
CINDY HEUER • CINDY TAYLOR • COLLEEN KASSMAN • CORRIE EDLING • COURTNEY HAWKINS
CRISTI WITT • DANA ELDER • DANA SPENCE • DANAE BURNS • DANIELLE JOHNSON • DANIELLE ABBOTT
DANYELLE GENTRY • DAWN BROWN • DAWN RACK • DEANA BOTTOMLEY • DEANN CHAMPAGNE
DEB WIEBERDINK • DEBBIE KOBERNICK • DEBBIE ZAMPETTI • DEBBIE HETHERINGTON
DEBORAH ROBERGE • DIANA WELLS • DIANE LANDEN • DONNA RUNION • DONNA DUARTE
DOTTIE BALLAGH • EILEEN MUELLER • ELLEN CASTELLI • EMILY BAKER • ERIN BROWN • ERIN SELLERS
ERIN JOHANSEN • FALLON JOHNSON • FLORBELA BRANCO • GILLIAN SMITH • GLORIA STERN
GRACE GAJDOS • GRETCHEN MANMILLER • HEATHER COX • HEATHER GLASS • HEATHER BELL
HEATHER BEARD • HEIDI HAGBERG • HEIDI GRAY • HOLLEY COX • HOLLY RUDDER • HOLLY BOSMAN
HOPE SHORTT • JA THOMS • JACKIE GERBERS • JACKIE DAVIDSON • JACY MASK • JAMI OYSTER
JAMIE BEELER • JANELLE DUPEE • JANELLE BENES • JANET BYERS • JEN ONEGLIA • JENNA BRANDES
JENNIFER CORNELL • JENNIFER WESSNER • JENNIFER WESTERHOFF • JENNIFER LOVELADY
JENNIFER TYLER • JENNIFER SMITH • JENNIFER AYCOCK • JENNIFER SKONOVD • JENNIFER LASKEY
JENNIFER ARENS • JENNIFER GARNER • JENNY HILLENBURG • JENNY WIEST • JENNY KILLEN
JESSICA KREMER • JESSICA FEAGLEY • JILL MULHOLLAND • JILL O'GORMAN • JODI DONNELLY
JOELLEN MARTIN • JONET GREENFIELD • JOSIE DENMAN • JUDI LANZONE • JULIA SLIKE • JULIE RABY
JULIE RAY • JULIE LEEDS • JULIE SEARS • JULIE STEVENSON • JULIE TILLER • JULIE MORGAN

JULIEANNA HOFFMAN-JUAREZ • KAINE STORY • KARA SCHMIDT • KARA YODER • KAREN ANTONAITIS
KAREN ROGERS • KARI SHUMAKER • KATHY PLANTON • KATIE RICHARDS • KATIE COTE
KELLI WHITMIRE • KELLY RICKETTS • KELLY LIVVIX • KELLY SMITH • KENDRA SCHMIT • KERRIE EARLY
KIM WEAVER • KIM MERCK • KIM KEIM • KIM RODDY • KIM JOHNSON • KIMBERLY STAPLES
KIRSTIN TRACY • KIRSTIN GREGURICH • KRISSY WALKER • KRISTA LUCE • KRISTEN BRININSTOOL
KRISTIN SCHAFER • KRISTIN CHRISTENSEN • KRISTINA OGURCAK • KRISTINE HAYS • KRISTY JOOS
KRYSTAL BLACKE • LARA LUDWICK • LAURA SEXSON • LAURA NEISWONGER • LAURA CLOUSE
LAUREL HUTSELL • LAURIE COPEMAN • LEAH GEORGE • LEAH KREIDERMACHER • LEIGH BOATWRIGHT
LESLIE MCKEE • LIBBY AULENBACH • LINDA PEDERSEN • LINDA COMPTON • LINDSAY TANNER
LINDSAY O'CONNOR • LINDSAY KAHL • LINDSEY BULLARD • LISA WOOD • LISA HARVEY
LISA NIEDERBERGER • LISA WITHERITE • LISA CASH • LISA WALLACE • LISA LOFTIS • LISA WINKLEMAN
LISA SMITH • LIZ TORGERSON • LIZ MARTINSON • LIZZY FONTAINE • LOIS BORKHOLDER
LORI BENSELER • LORI BUSH • LORI MILLER • LORI SORENSEN • LORI REDDINGER • LORI FORD
LORI MARTIN • LYDIANN KING • LYN DOWNEY • LYNN PFOST • LYNN MCCUTCHEON • LYNN STOWMAN
MAGGIE MCLAUGHLIN • MANDIE STUDER • MARCI SNIVELY • MARGIE COOK • MARIEKAN MARTIN
MARLENA ROUDA • MARSHA DIXON • MARTA GUINN • MEGAN BRYSON • MEGAN ARCHIBALD
MELANIE POTTER • MELINDA HUGHES-RORAPAUGH • MELISSA KAULE • MELISSA DAVIS
MELISSA LANG • MELISSA KARNOWSKI • MICHELLE TARPLEY • MICHELLE WERTH • MICHELLE KISER
MIRANDA PERAZZO • MISSY TUCKER-SIMMEN • MISTY THOMAS • MISTY ELLIOTT • MONICA ADDISON
MONIKA ENGEL • NADINE WILLEMSE • NEELY BASICH • NIKKI HUFFMAN • NIKKI HOLLAND
NIKKIE GLATT • PAM GUNTER • PAULA MCCREA • PEGGY GERHARDT • RACHEL CATOE
REBECCA HIGGINS • REBECCA BRIDLE • REYNE GALEY • ROBYN WHITE • SAMANTHA THOMPSON
SANDRA DICKENS • SANDY IRWIN • SARAH CARPER • SARAH COLTON • SARAH BAKER
SARAH HARDY • SARAH FARNSWORTH • SARAH LAMMERT • SARAH OVERMAN • SHALANE KOON
SHAUNA BIGGERSTAFF • SHELLEY HEILE • SHELRENA PRUITT • SHERI BANWART • STACEY HAAS
STACEY CARR • STACY KUTNER • STASI PRECOUR • STEFANIE NAILLON • STORMY MILLER • SUE SALERNO
SUSAN SULLIVAN • SUSAN HILDEBRAND • SUSAN EFKEN • SUZANNE HUDSON • SUZANNE KING
TABITHA FISHER • TAMMY WELLS • TAMMY AUSTIN • TAMMY C. PULSIFER • TANDY SCHWAIGER
TARA BALL • TARA BERRY • TERESA SIMMONS • TERI PERROTT • TERRY BUETZOW
TIFFANY WELLINGHOFF • TINA GADE-LIEB • TRACI ROTTMANN • TRACY BROOKSHIRE • TRACY COLBERT
TYREE TOOHEY • VICKI JAMES • VICKIE WITT • WENDI SUMNER

EXTENDED AUTHOR BIO

Cindy Monroe is a champion of women and a pioneer of opportunity. Guided by a vision of empowering women to do and be more for themselves and their families, she has used her entrepreneurial success to open doors for women of all backgrounds to establish and build their own businesses through Thirty-One, the direct sales company she founded with friends. She is a leader, mentor, and teacher, arming women with an opportunity for personal growth and increased self-confidence, as well as a vehicle to effect change inside and outside of their homes.

Cindy's fierce faith, family focus, and authentic passion for changing lives give her a platform to lead others toward the future every woman wants. And she does so by illustrating a vision, demonstrating tireless commitment, and believing in women, even when they don't believe in themselves.

Thirty-One offers exclusive, on-trend handbags, accessories, and organizational solutions for in the home and on the go. Most Thirty-One products can be personalized, enabling customers to create unique gifts and keepsakes.